To Feel as Our Ancestors Did

To Feel as Our Ancestors Did

COLLECTING
AND PERFORMING
ORAL HISTORIES

Daniel A. Kelin II

HEINEMANN
Portsmouth, NH

Heinemann
A division of Reed Elsevier Inc.
361 Hanover Street
Portsmouth, NH 03801–3912
www.heinemann.com

Offices and agents throughout the world

Library of Congress Cataloging-in-Publication Data
Kelin, Daniel A.
 To feel as our ancestors did : collecting and performing oral histories / Daniel A. Kelin II.
  p. cm.
 Includes bibliographical references and index.
 ISBN 0-325-00686-5 (alk. paper)
  1. Drama in education. 2. Drama—Study and teaching. 3. Oral history. I. Title.
PN3171.K34 2005
371.39'9—dc22   2004024035

Editor: Lisa A. Barnett
Production editor: Sonja S. Chapman
Cover design: Jenny Jensen Greenleaf
Compositor: Reuben Kantor, QEP Design
Manufacturing: Steve Bernier

Printed in the United States of America on acid-free paper

09   08   07   06   05   DA   1   2   3   4   5

To my own "history," my parents and grandparents

Contents

Acknowledgments

The initial idea for this combination of oral history and drama wasn't even mine. It began with a telephone call seeking advice. During the call I mentioned my interest in such a project. My thanks to Kahala Elementary School for giving me the opportunity to begin.

Without the consistent financial support of the Rev. Takie Okumura Family Fund through the Hawai'i Community Foundation, the idea would have ended after its first year. Most particularly I offer many deep mahalos to Karen Misaki for working so hard to keep the funds flowing.

Plenty of people contributed to the defining and refining of the project. First, of course, are all the students. Their enthusiasm, skepticism, questions, comments, and honest openness kept the process sharp, worthwhile, and vibrant. Several colleagues did the same. I will never be able to offer enough thanks to Tracy Hirsch, Kenny and Chizuko Endo, Calvin Hoe, Naoko Mayeshiba, Peter Rockford-Espiritu, Y York, Tara Ziegler, Cheryl Treiber-Kawaoka, and Warren Nishimoto of the University of Hawai'i Center for Oral History. I also offer sincere thanks to James McCarthy, Kristi Lynn Johnson, Peggy Hunt, and Karen Wright. Valuable support also came from the sidelines at Honolulu Theatre for Youth. None of this would have been possible without Jane Campbell and Mark Lutwak.

I especially wish to acknowledge the support, enthusiasm, and nice words of the many school teachers and principals who participated, Richard Crislip, Helen Kishi, JoAnn Hirayasu, Muriel Watanabe, Terry Jeminez, Louise Cayetano, Diane Aoki, Jodee Schmidt-Young, Ellory Gallanto, Linda Kamiyama, and Elsie Kobayashi.

Finally, and most recently, my thanks to Heinemann, most particularly to Lisa Barnett for a long haul of support, patience, and encouragement.

Introduction

History is what we all need to learn because it tells about the world and wonderful things that have happened.
—SIXTH GRADER, WAHIAWA

If drama wasn't invented there wouldn't be talking.
—SIXTH GRADER, KALIHI

There is nothing like a good story. Our lives are based around stories, from bedtime stories when we are young to daily anecdotes about the silly events we have seen or embarrassed ourselves with to the stories we use to illustrate points or educate our students. Increasing evidence points to stories playing a key role in our development as communicators, readers, and writers. In addition, a key aspect of that development is sharing stories of ourselves.

Each of us is full of stories. Every day we live the story of our lives, from losing our keys to losing a loved one, from getting married to getting the perfect gift. By sharing these stories, we have the chance to put our lives into perspective. By listening to the stories of others, we validate their experience and life. By preserving the stories we share and hear, our family, heritage, and culture can live forever.

Our communities are full of surprising stories. Imagine talking to the elderly man next door and discovering that when he was a boy a Japanese Zero Airplane crashed right in his backyard. And that's the backyard connected to yours! Suddenly you look at the backyard as something more impressive than a field of grass and vegetables. The yard, the community, becomes a place for discovery and learning.

Our stories of self, community, and heritage have so much to offer us, yet often the books we read and the stories we study in school are not connected to our community and us. Certainly, the stories of other places can surprise, enthrall, and educate us, but we should not miss the significant history of our own community.

Because you most likely live where your ancestors lived, it shapes who you are. It also holds the key to your past. What your ancestors did is what you are.

—SIXTH GRADER, WAHIAWA

To educate the whole child requires much more than the time spent in class. However, unless families, the community, and the young people themselves come to see the important part they play in young peoples' learning, then education will be less about the children and more about them being forced to remember "what's good for them" or "what's good for their future."

If young people themselves are going to significantly contribute to their own education, then they need to be given the opportunity to ask questions, make choices, and take risks that, succeed or fail, offer them the chance to discover the answers for themselves. Teachers should offer opportunities to learn. Moreover, the learning should be about discovery. To increase young people's interest in learning, what they learn should not always be dictated to them. They need to learn how to learn. Moreover, they should drive the process of learning.

In our technology-based society, young people spend more time watching TV and videos; their minds are filled with images and language from a world not their own. These children become integrated into a homogenized popular culture, and they lose connection with the past, culture, and heritage that have brought them to this point in time.

A key to offsetting this loss is the imagination. There is no question that when our imaginations are engaged, we become very attentive. Young people crave active engagement. They want to get up and do, to be involved. They grow up playacting, learning about the world by imagining themselves in a variety of roles, relationships, and situations. Drama education builds on the way young people process the world, placing them at the center of the process. They can be other people, go to other places and times. Young people learn through drama because the learning is about them.

Drama challenges children to be mentally, emotionally, and physically involved. Drama gets participants to think, imagine, problem-solve, and understand. Drama is about human behavior and interaction, therefore incorporating basic life skills including communication skills (both oral and written), working well with others, risk-taking, reflection, evaluation, and leadership qualities. Drama involves all students simultaneously, challenging them to work together to help and learn from each other. Each child contributes to the process in significant ways. All of the students challenge themselves, each to his own degree of comfort.

Drama education immerses young people in the story or event actively. Placed "in character," the young people relate to and invest in the character and situation. Seeing a historical event through the eyes of the characters prepares the young participants for rich and thoughtful discussions. This personal engagement empowers young people, developing communication and problem-solving and interpersonal skills.

The memory of such explorations and performances stay with young people longer than memorized facts. As they have lived the situation, they are in a position to draw their own conclusions about the events and the characters. Their investment and emotional engagement in the event help them understand the situation better, preparing them for rich discussions about the event and how it connects to or affects our own world.

> I think learning History is important. Because of History we are free from Britain.
>
> —SIXTH GRADER, WAHIAWA

"Drama" and "Theatre"

Throughout this book, I separate the terms *drama* and *theatre* in the way others use *process* and *product*. Drama, in this vocabulary, is a process of exploration not necessarily involving a performance. It is a physically, emotionally, intellectually engaging process that helps young people discover, connect to, and safely explore a wide range of subjects. Certainly the skills of the actor are utilized, but not as the focus of the process. What is important is what the participants learn, not what an audience may gain. Theatre is an event—a performance. Teaching theatre skills is teaching young people how to be performers, how to speak and move and present themselves, and at a more advanced level, how to be actors.

1

Overview and Timeline

We invited different guests into the classroom so we could interview them. After we interviewed the guests we had to choose which story, we wanted to be in. Then we decided which roles we wanted to play. After we told the teacher what we wanted to be we made tableaus of some of the scenes. Then we showed the class our tableau and we took suggestions and made it better. When it got real good we brought it to life and made it better and better. When we were close to finishing the scenes, the movement lady came in and helped us work on our movement scenes. After that, some kids went to learn taiko drums and Hawai'ian instruments. When they were done learning, we worked on the scene transitions. When we were finished with that we went to the cafeteria and worked on the class transitions. Then we did the play.

—SIXTH GRADER, KANE'OHE

The *To Feel as Our Ancestors Did* model involves upper elementary and middle school <u>students in collecting oral histories and developing them into living history presentations.</u> The model is an intense, daily process that keeps students' attention on exploring, understanding, and shaping the oral history stories through a combination of drama techniques, music, movement, and performance. Students are deeply immersed in meaningful stories through a rich process, which brings together a community in celebration of itself, and its young people. Little focus is placed on sets, lights, costumes, and other production values.

The process strives to:

- offer students the opportunity to discover and explore the stories of their culturally diverse backgrounds, preserving family stories and history;
- use the drama process and theatre experience to explore and present oral histories;
- enhance students' oral and written communication skills;
- encourage students to appreciate the power of stories to instill pride in one's self, family, community and heritage;
- create strong ties between families, the community, and the school;
- encourage students to see the community as a place of learning.

Birth of the Idea

To Feel as Our Ancestors Did began as a partnership between Honolulu Theatre for Youth (HTY) and Kahala Elementary School under a Hawai'i State Department of Education Innovation and Incentive Grant. Due to the success of and excitement generated by that partnership, each year, for several years, Honolulu Theatre for Youth (HTY) partnered with a different elementary school to immerse upper elementary students in the unique history of each school's community through drama and theatre. The annual project (originally titled "Communal and Cultural Understandings") was primarily supported by grants from the Rev. Takie Okumura Family Fund with other local grantors. Throughout this book are many letters and excerpts from journals of the students and teachers involved in those partnerships.

> *Our class is more willing to perform. Before we were lazy and quiet. After the fact, we were so enthusiastic and prepared. We now know how to project and focus. I think throughout the year we put our lessons together and realized the importance of this play. That was probably why we were so outstanding! So, our class has changed our entire personalities, feelings, and opinions about acting in general. A lot of us perform now instead of sitting back and relaxing.*
> —SIXTH GRADER, KALIHI

Philosophy

Young people are often put into plays under the idea that children are "natural actors" and it should be quick and easy to create a performance. However, young people are not truly "actors," they are explorers (and occasionally show-offs!). They play out situations to understand them, to experiment with roles they may play later in life. It is a personal learning process.

Putting young people on stage is different from young people playing out life situations. They do not innately understand the concept of performing for an audience. They do not innately grasp the concept that an audience cannot hear them if they are too soft-spoken (after all, they can hear themselves). They do not naturally realize that if they turn their backs toward the audience or bunch up in tight groups with their peers on the stage, the audience cannot see them. They are focused on their own exploration.

For young people to make the leap from exploring to performing requires one very important step: understanding. Young people *must* be given sufficient time to understand what it is they will be performing, and only then can they grasp the concepts of projection, enunciation, and relating to an audience. The potential young performers must have the time to explore the material in their own fashion. They need the time to find their own words and their own actions to accompany them. Once they understand the material, they can understand the theatrical concepts of reaching an audience.

To rush this process is to cheat the young people. Certainly, they can be made to look good on stage and certainly parents and relatives will love them for it. However, if they have not taken charge of the process and their handiwork, then they have not learned. They have had fun, they have gained some glory, but the learning has not reached its full potential. It is equivalent to giving young people the answers to an upcoming test to ensure they do well on it.

Understanding takes time and patience, something young people and adults both might run out of during the process. But to see it through is to give young people the unique chance to take full ownership of the process, and more than likely to impress everyone who comes to see the product that much more.

The process, as outlined in this book, is structured to engage and involve students at every step. They are given the chance to choose what to explore and how to explore it. They choose how involved they are, what parts they should play, and how to best shape their involvement. By involving them in the oral history interviews, choosing the material to explore, devising the scenes and short plays, creating and performing the stories, characters, music, and movement, and sharing their learning with peers, families, and the community, the young participants see how learning works from their interest and in their favor. Actively engaged through drama, students take ownership of the process and thus their own learning.

When the learning comes from and is about the students, their investment is deep. When they see themselves in the learning, see how it is useful to them and see how they benefit from it, they become more interested in learning. This understanding can then be applied to other subjects. Using drama to explore and perform stories of family, community, and heritage, young people are immersed in their own past. Say, for example, a class chooses the topic of World War II in America. Interviewing grandparents who grew up during the war gives young people firsthand experience with how the war affected people and especially children.

The learning does not stop there, however. As the students create the scenes and short plays, they will want to find out more about the time period and how people lived. They will be motivated to do research on the war, finding out about food, transportation, communication, in order to set a context for their drama explorations.

By offering students the time and process for truly understanding, the learning can be endless.

Overview of the Process

As outlined in this book, the model has many parts. However, not every part is essential to a successful process. Following is a brief introduction to each step of the process covered in this book. The steps labeled with asterisks (*) are the recommended essential steps to offer students a full experience for exploring and creating scenes or short plays from personally collected oral histories. The other steps can be added in any combination as desired or deemed useful for the particular class, school, or group of participating students.

*Project Theme**

> Teachers and/or students choose a school-specific or curriculum-connected theme to focus the oral history interviews, scenes, and short plays. General themes offer the greatest possibilities (i.e., "Triumphs and Tragedies"). Young people are particularly interested in stories of the oral history informants' childhood (i.e., "Back in My Younger Days").

*Drama Skill-Building**

> Students explore and experiment with basic drama techniques, such as ensemble, tableau, pantomime, and improvisation, building a common drama vocabulary that will be applied in both the devising sequence and rehearsal process steps.

Interview Skill-Building

> Students experiment with, explore, and discuss how to develop questions and conduct effective interviews by conducting mock interviews with fellow students and the project teacher(s) and drama instructor(s).

Collecting Oral Histories*

Students conduct interviews with and record oral histories of family members, relatives, neighbors, or community members to find engaging and unique stories about their own community or family heritage.

Devising Sequence*

Students apply the techniques they learned in the drama skill-building step to explore and create scenes and short plays from the collected oral histories.

Music and Movement Workshops

Students learn to employ a variety of instruments, using the music to create mood for the scenes and transitions between stories. Students develop a basic movement vocabulary to imagine and devise ways to add movement to their scenes.

Design and Production

The drama instructor coordinates the design and building of simple props, costumes, and sets with the teachers, community/family volunteers, or with the students themselves. The elements are designed to support the imaginative exploration of the process. This keeps the students' and audiences' focus on the scenes, not the "stuff," and keeps control over the size of the performance (and its costs).

Rehearsal Process*

• *Individual Rehearsals*

Individual classes polish their devised scenes and short plays, adding supporting elements, including music, movement, props, set(s), or costume pieces and/or other students.

• *Joint Rehearsals*

When several classes are performing together, the classes develop transitions that will link their presentations for the performance. Students fine-tune basic performance skills.

Family Night Workshop

Parents are introduced to the process and philosophy of the project in a hands-on workshop. With their children, the parents experiment with some of the drama techniques.

Performances*

Classes share their presentations with the school and community.

Project Assessment

A simple survey is conducted; student journals and teacher observation forms track changes in attitude, knowledge, and understanding of the students.

- *Pre- and Postsurveys*

  Simple surveys track changes in student attitude toward history, elders, drama, and their own sense of self.

- *Student Journals*

  Students keep regular journals of thoughts and reactions to workshops, evaluations of their own participation, and constructive criticism of other individuals and groups within their class.

- *Teacher/Artist Observation Forms*

  The teacher and visiting artists regularly record their observations of individual student and whole-class development.

- *Postevaluation Guide*

  The drama instructor and classroom teacher evaluate the overall achievements of the students and class.

- *Postproject Reflection and Evaluation*

  Students and teachers assess what they learned about themselves, their peers, their community, drama, and history through structured activities and questions.

Role of Specialists and Teacher

Hopefully this book offers drama specialists and classroom teachers enough philosophy, insight, information, and resources to work together to implement the *To Feel as Our Ancestors Did* process at some level. If several classes or whole grade levels are involved, some of the steps in the process might be shared among participating teachers, as teachers often have additional skills that might benefit the process. Certainly drawing on the talents of the school's music teacher or cultural specialist, if one is available, will enrich the process.

.   The classroom teacher should be the one coordinating and scheduling the interviews, as the personal interaction with the interviewee can make a great deal of difference in how the interviews play out. This personal connection will also pay off when the time comes for the performances, as inviting the interviewees to the performances is a valuable part of validating and celebrating the creative work of the students.

Role of Visiting Artists

The opportunity to involve the greater community outside of the school should not be missed. With larger-scale versions of this process, outside talent will not only deepen the process but also offer students the chance to see the community as a valuable place for learning.

Bringing in artists to assist with the music and movement can be an enriching and rewarding process for the students as well as participating teacher. Visiting artists can help the teacher and students explore possibilities that might not otherwise have occurred to them. In addition, artists are good at breaking open the process, guiding students away from overly realistic and linear ways of thinking that will result in unique and exciting manners of expression.

Adventurous teachers could also learn from the visiting artists' sessions—learning that can be applied to later steps in the process.

Timeline Considerations for the Process

Instead of a timetable prescribing the length and size of the process and duration of each step, this book introduces interested educators, administrators, and teaching artists to the how and why of the process, encouraging experimentation and exploration. The book is a guide through a varied and rich process of engaging whole classrooms of students to be actively involved in imagining, exploring, creating, and performing scenes and short plays from personally collected oral histories. The process ensures that young participants have a chance to explore, understand, and apply learning at each step. It is also a process that encourages and supports every student's contribution to the process, in ways that are both comfortable for and challenging to each individual student.

The original project model, as developed and implemented by HTY, generally involved six classes and lasted anywhere between ten and fifteen weeks, with individual classes meeting every day for sessions of forty-five to sixty minutes. The intent was to create a sustained involvement by the young participants, keeping their focus on consistently building on their efforts.

It is well noted, however, that this is a lot of time for a class or school to give over to a single project, especially given the growing demands on schools and teachers. However, one of the many useful features of this model is its potential to expand or contract to fit the interests or needs of a particular class or school. The whole process could conceivably occur within a single month, depending on the number of oral history stories chosen and the complexity of the scenes or short plays. As the process is driven by choices, students, teachers, classes, or schools can determine the necessity and size of each part of the process.

Another useful feature is the model's capacity to augment and integrate other core curricula areas, from physical education to language arts to social studies. This ensures that if a motivated class or school wishes to make a full-fledged go at the entire process as outlined in the book, the class or school could make this project a central course of study during a school year, with each part of the curriculum focused around the history of the school's surrounding community. In addition to the culminating performance(s), classes or schools might create i-movie documentaries of the process, self-published books of the oral histories, or parent night displays of project pictures and related research, or even use the project as a jumping-off place for the annual national History Day project.

The key to determining the overall length of the process is knowing the participating students. The drama skill-building section (Chapter 2) is intended to offer students a chance to experiment with how drama works and to become comfortable with the techniques needed to create original scenes and short plays. If the students feel comfortable with creating and presenting, then less time should be spent on that particular section of the project. In like fashion, if the students take to any step of the process with ease and comfort, then it is not necessary to spend as much time on that particular step in the process.

The devising and rehearsal sections (Chapters 5 and 8) of the project expand and contract according to how many oral history stories are chosen or how long the class or school hopes the culmination to be. If a whole class works together on one story (such as the Philippine World War II story outlined in Chapter 5), the class could conceivably create a brief series of scenes lasting just ten minutes in as little as a couple of weeks. If the same class decides to tell the story by combining a series of six to ten tableaux (frozen images), narration, and a little accompanying music, the process could be completed in a week.

How much is created should not be the goal. How successfully students relate to the material and make it their own is the goal. When students conduct the interviews, then choose the oral history stories with which they wish to work, the process is already well along the way. Discussing the most effective ways to explore and create scenes or short plays from the stories (Should the stories be fully realized into scenes or short plays or be a series of simple vignettes or narrative-defined pantomimes or tableaux?) helps takes the process of understanding to another level.

Keeping class options open and choosing the most personally interesting or poignant ways to shape the oral history stories in performance pieces, allows for a lot of leeway with the time frame for the overall project.

The process is the focus and the culmination is a sharing of students' achievements made during the process. Each day of the project should be an adventure of exploration and discovery. The crucial point here is that whatever the length, the process must serve and build from the needs of the students. If at any time an educator finds herself saying "If the student(s) would just say this or that, then the scene would be so much better," or "It would be much easier for the students if I just wrote out the lines to say, so they could just concentrate on giving a good performance" or any statements remotely like these, it signals the end of the process for the young people. As soon as an adult tells a student what to do or say, then the young person's investment in the process lessens. If the young participants do not understand or are having a hard time with any step in the process, that step should have more time dedicated to it.

Following are suggestions to consider when deciding on a potential timeline and the length of each of the steps in the process.

Project Theme

This should be the first step in the process. Creating a focus for the overall project gives every step a clear purpose and guides the oral history interviews and the choice of the oral history stories to explore and dramatize.

Drama Skill-Building, Interview Skill-Building, and the Interviews

The order of these three steps is flexible. Having the students prepare for and conduct the interviews before exploring and learning drama techniques helps focus their attention on why the drama techniques are necessary. However, by conducting the drama sessions first, students build an excitement for conducting the interviews, knowing the process they will be using to explore the stories. They may also have a better understanding of what makes a good story and be more astute in the interviews. For this reason, each of the drama skill-building and interview skill-building steps have built into them explorations and discussions of stories.

This is an important point. Although young people do recognize what kinds of stories interest them, understanding what makes a good story to dramatize is a different situation. Experience teaches me that students respond to that which is funny or action-oriented, not yet fully appreciating the subtleties of character, character intention, and conflict. Focusing each of these steps on stories and storying is useful for both the students and the overall process.

Drama Skill-Building

At whatever point in the process the drama skill-building step is implemented, the focus should be on the students learning to use the skills and techniques they will apply in the devising sequence step. The process suggested in this book consists of two parts: learning basic drama techniques and experimenting with applying those techniques to an original story developed by the students. Each is important to students' ability to take control of the process; however, the amount of time needed for students to understand and feel comfortable with the techniques is flexible.

In five days of daily sessions, students can simultaneously learn the basic drama techniques while applying them to an original story they develop. In ten to fifteen days of daily sessions, participants more deeply explore the skills and techniques needed to dramatize the oral history stories, with the fifteen-day plan allowing more time for the students to develop into a strong working ensemble.

In Chapter 2 (Drama Skill-Building), there are two sample lesson plans: a ten- and a fifteen-day plan. Drama instructors should reformat, lengthening or shortening the lesson plans, to focus on whatever skills are deemed necessary or useful for the participating students.

Interview Skill-Building

If students are not schooled in asking questions, then this step is an important one. As outlined in the interview skill-building chapter (Chapter 3), there are particular kinds of questions and ways to ask them that will result in oral history stories rich with possibilities for exploration and dramatization. The chapter details a three-session sample lesson plan that repeats the process of asking questions several times to ensure students truly understand; after all, they generally get only one opportunity to conduct an interview. The chapter offers ways to explore other skills as well, such as learning to listen.

As with each step in the process, the number and length of these sessions should fit the particular needs of the students.

Collecting Oral Histories

The *To Feel as Our Ancestors Did* process could be used with a wide range of stories, from made-up classroom stories to published literature. However, what makes this process unique is the focus on oral histories. A well-orchestrated forty-five- to sixty-minute interview will produce more than enough material from which to draw. To be well orchestrated, teachers need to spend time on preparing the interview beyond just asking someone to be interviewed. It is important that the teacher conduct a preinterview to prepare the interviewee for the kinds of questions the students might focus on and to discover the range of topics best suited to the particular interviewee.

Devising Sequence

The devising sequence is the core of the entire process. Every step before this prepares for the devising, while every step after this one refines and shapes the work of this step. This is where the time for understanding is needed. The devising sequence should solidify the students' contributions, making it clear to themselves and others that their work is the focus of the process. Students should take control.

If possible, the length of time spent devising should be flexible. The longer and more complex the oral history stories are, the longer the process will be to dramatize them. In addition, it should be remembered that young people need time to first understand the characters and story they are working on before they become completely comfortable with fully dramatizing them.

At the very least, if the scene(s) being developed consists mostly of simple still images and/or simple pantomimes accompanied primarily by narration or if the participating students are very comfortable with working with improvisation, a week of daily sessions should be set aside.

When scheduling a particular period of time for the whole process, allow a good week of devising time (every day for about an hour a day) for each individual scene within a story. (See Chapter 5 for a more complete understanding of scenes.)

Music and Movement Workshops

Music—The scenes or short plays benefit from the addition of simple musical accompaniment. With a handful of "found object" percussive instruments, most students can easily create some sort of musical accompaniment or sound effects support for a scene or short play with little need for additional sessions.

If a class or school decides to enrich the students' experience with musical workshops, then offering students at least a few sessions to become comfortable with the basics of playing a simple instrument is necessary. This will give them enough knowledge to suggest ways to enrich the scenes and short plays with their newly gained musical skills (combined with a little imaginative experimentation).

The instruments suggested in this book are Japanese taiko drums and Hawai'ian nose flutes. These instruments were originally chosen in the Hawai'i project as they connected to the cultural heritage of many of the students involved. However, in my experience, most students find these instruments simple to learn and exciting to play. Instructions detailing how to build simple versions of these instruments are included in the appendices.

It is not necessary, of course, for students to build instruments. Any percussive instrument can add to the process, as can recorders, a standard instrument in many music classes and schools.

Whatever the choice, students should learn and begin using the instruments during the devising sequence step, in order to organically involve the music in the scenes being developed.

Movement—The scenes or short plays can also benefit from the addition of simple movement sequences. This does not necessarily mean dance sequences, rather physical representations of ideas or events (such as airplanes, fires, rivers, races, or sports events). Given a few imaginative props (blue cloth for water, rope to define the shape of vehicles), students can easily imagine and create simple movement sequences to augment their scene or short play with little need for additional sessions.

If a class or school decides to enrich the students' experience with movement workshops, then offering students a few sessions to become comfortable with a range of movement is necessary. This will give them enough knowledge to suggest ways to enrich the scenes and short plays with their newly gained movement skills (again, combined with a little imaginative experimentation).

Whatever the choice, students should experiment with or learn movement during the devising sequence step in order to organically involve the movement in the scenes being developed.

Rehearsal Process

Before moving on to the rehearsal process, students should have a clear understanding of the storyline or sequence of the scenes or short plays as well as have generated enough dialogue and action in the devising sequence step to be clearly communicating the oral history stories. The rehearsal process then focuses on refining and defining the scenes and short plays that have been devised.

As with the devising sequence step, this process is best if kept flexible. However, a good rule of thumb is planning for a rehearsal process of approximately half to two-thirds the length of the devising sequence step.

Individual Rehearsals—Individual rehearsals are those rehearsals focused on a single class. The time guidelines stated above should be adequate for creating tight, focused scenes.

The rehearsal should primarily focus on the content of the scenes, not on performance skills. Enunciation and projection should be left until the last few days of rehearsal (or the joint rehearsals if more than one class is participating), when the excitement is growing and the students are truly concerned with how their audience will react to the scenes and short plays. Focusing too quickly on performance skills undercuts the students' need to understand and take control of the content of the scenes and short plays.

Joint Rehearsals—The joint rehearsals bring together the classes sharing a performance. This process need happen only a few days before the performance and should focus primarily on perfecting performance skills, creating simple transitions between the individual class presentations, and staging a curtain call for the groups.

If the classes each have a fifteen- to twenty-minute presentation, then these joint rehearsals should be about two hours in length. This gives time to practice performance skills and run through the scenes and short plays each day, as well as dedicate time to create and practice the transitions on one day and stage and practice the curtain call on another. Three to four consecutive days of joint rehearsals just before the performances should be plenty.

Family Night Workshop

Very little time is needed for this special workshop. However, the rewards are immense. In a single evening's session of forty-five to sixty minutes, parents gain a significant understanding of the process their children are experiencing. They will also become more astute at seeing how much the students have contributed to and gained from the process while watching the performances.

Design and Production

Many school-based productions feature homemade, parent-designed sets and costumes, lending an atmosphere of theatricality to the student production. *To Feel as Our Ancestors Did* focuses more on the process of creation than on the presentation. Little to no emphasis should be put on production values except to create a space for exploration. Using a select number of chairs, stools, and/or small benches as the set pieces focuses attention on the students and emphasizes the imaginative exploration of the process. In a similar fashion, having the students wear black T-shirts, jeans, and sneakers focuses attention on their efforts, not on their clothes.

Performances

At the end of the process, students should have the opportunity to share their creations. The performance should reflect the process. The shorter the process and the smaller the presentation, the more informal the performance should be. Classes might share with each other, other classes in the school, the entire school, parents, and/or the greater community.

Project Assessment

Students fill out student surveys anonymously just before the process begins and again just after the whole process has finished. Comparing the results gives a good overview of the change in attitude and understanding of the class or group as a whole.

Throughout, the students should keep regular journals, documenting their growth, feelings, and learning at each step of the process. Giving students ten to fifteen minutes to write in their journals immediately after a session focuses their thoughts and offers them a chance to evaluate themselves and set goals for future sessions.

Benefiting From Other Resources

Few of us work in isolation, whether we live on an island or not. Many intelligent and gifted people have written books on process drama, theatre, interviewing, and oral history that have influenced the development of this particular process in many ways. To avoid duplicating myself, I leave the names of these various books to the Bibliography, but I do wish to point out one in particular.

The work I do, as reflected in this book, is heavily influenced by drama. The whole oral history in performance project began as a way to increase the amount of time the HTY drama education staff spent in direct contact with students. At the very beginning, the oral history gathering and interviews were steps that the HTY staff had little to do with, trusting that the teachers would take care of those. However, as we repeated the project, we found ourselves increasingly interested in arranging and conducting the oral history interviews. One wonderfully rich book that guided our efforts is Paula Rogovin's *Classroom Interviews: A World of Learning.* I cannot recommend it enough to those interested in spending more time with interviews and oral histories.

2

Drama Skill-Building

I know that Drama is a way of communicating and learning how to work with other people and to work as a team and participating.
—SIXTH GRADER, KALIHI

Learning drama is important because it lets you create an idea about how your life is going to be.
—SIXTH GRADER, KALIHI

AT A GLANCE

Students explore and experiment with basic drama techniques, such as ensemble, tableau, pantomime, and improvisation, building a common drama vocabulary that will be applied in both the devising sequence step and rehearsal process.

GOALS/OBJECTIVES

- to introduce students and teachers to a wide variety of drama techniques and strategies
- to introduce students to the tools needed to create scenes and short plays from the oral history material
- to enhance students' oral communication skills
- to develop a common drama vocabulary

Figure 2–1.
A student-created web demonstrating her understanding of drama.

- to develop a supportive atmosphere in which students feel comfortable sharing
- to build working ensembles within each class

INSIGHT

I really liked it when you let us pick which play we wanted to be in because other drama teachers would have just said you play this part and you play that part. Plus you also let us say what we wanted to say not this is your line memorize it.

—SIXTH GRADER, KANEʻOHE

Exploring Drama Techniques

There is a defined set of techniques that will be used throughout this process. These techniques are the basic building blocks of drama and theatre. Taken as a whole, these techniques develop students' use of their bodies, voices, and imaginations. The sample ten- and fifteen-day drama lesson plans outlined at the end of this chapter build slowly, exercising students' developing skills and challenging them to take more control of the process, exploring how to create and shape scenes and short plays improvisationally.

First students learn what the drama techniques are, exploring the techniques through simple and quick exercises and activities, and next they practice applying the techniques in informal situations and scenes. Finally, in the devising sequence step, students put the techniques into action, transforming the collected oral histories into scenes and short plays.

The ultimate achievement is to have the students take control of the process. The instructor should only help guide the work through questions that spur the students on to solve problems and come up with solutions. They will not be able to do this without the right tools. This is where the drama techniques come in. With basic techniques, the students will be able to look at the oral history material and decide if they should make tableaux, explore the material through pantomime, or try to develop full characters through improvisation.

Drama skill-building is broken into four sections:

Warming Up to Drama/Building Ensemble

Young people need to play, explore, and build comfort with drama before they can be expected to create or perform. The first drama sessions should create an atmosphere of fun and open creative play, to reduce fear or trepidation. By starting with gamelike activities, students will come to see the more they involve themselves, the more fun it will be. At the same time, the focus should be firmly on the task at hand so students learn to focus energy and creativity, avoiding the temptation to use drama class to "show off."

Students should also develop a sense that everyone in the class is taking risks. Building trust requires a safe atmosphere in which students feel they can trust both the instructor and the other members of the class to be attentive, supportive, and responsive to ideas and suggestions. Students should come to understand how important it is to give ideas a try, without worrying that others will judge them for their attempts, be they effective or not.

The students should also find positive ways to work together, support each other, and problem-solve, as they will be called upon repeatedly to brainstorm, create, and develop scenes and short plays, something they cannot do without partners. The ensemble-building activities offer students the chance to exercise their understanding of collaboration and community. Even if the group is a class that has been together for a while, working in a drama setting is different from working in small groups on other projects. By exploring ensemble first through games, students discover the advantages to working well together. As these activities are explored, set aside a little time after each to discuss how the activities established a sense of teamwork and how teams were successful.

Developing Tools for Expression

The three basic tools of the performer are body, voice, and imagination. Fortunately, for most young people, imagination still plays a very strong role in their lives. Body and voice are a completely different matter. Students need time to work past the self-consciousness of using their bodies and voices as tools for expression. This series of exercises and activities intentionally begins with freeform movement, giving the students the opportunity to explore and shake loose the self-consciousness. The activities sustain an atmosphere of fun about the work, challenging students to explore the full range of possibilities with the body and voice, from the subtle to the ridiculous. Later when they work on "realistic" situations in drama class, the self-consciousness will be gone and students will be able to focus on becoming adept with the drama techniques.

In brief, the voice work mirrors the movement work. Exploring the possibilities of nonverbal vocal expression is more fun and eye-opening than being weighted down with techniques such as projection and enunciation. Those techniques will come later, when they truly have some meaning and use to the students.

Exploring Devising Techniques

The third section of drama skill-building is all about exploring the basic techniques used to create, structure, and shape oral history material into scenes, particularly tableau and improvisation. More in-depth discussion will be found in the sections outlining those specific techniques, but it is important to note that the fun should not be lost when exploring and learning to use these techniques. The drama sessions give students the chance to try out the techniques to see how they work and to understand how to become good at using them. As is inherent within practice, mistakes are meant to happen, because often we learn better that way. During this part of drama class the instructor should be guiding the students to create their own checklist for accomplishments. As they try the techniques, the students should be encouraged to recognize when the techniques work best and then apply that understanding to create the list. To aid in this process, a suggested checklist can be found in each of the individual sections. However, do not follow them verbatim. Use the opportunity for the students to truly become active learners by building their own lists, no matter how simple it might be.

Throughout this section, avoid focusing too much on the content of the explorations. Help the students learn how to use the techniques first.

Sharing and Building Stories

This last step is about practical application of the techniques being explored, still without losing the atmosphere of fun and exploration. Throughout the drama sessions, a discussion should be had about stories: what the students like about stories, what makes good stories, who to ask to find stories, and how to ask to get stories.

Paralleling these conversations and collections, students learn ways to use the drama techniques to imagine, create, develop, and informally act out an original class story. These activities expand on the skills the students have been developing in drama class and engage them for the first time in the process of shaping a story into dramatized scenes and short plays. Through this process, the students also discover the basic properties of a "good" story.

An option is to have students collect stories, both their own (based on personal memories) and those from family or other relatives. With these collected stories they apply the play-building process to shape the oral history material into scenes and short plays.

JOURNAL RESPONSE QUESTIONS

A list of potential questions follows. This list was developed over time and with students in Hawai'i. Use as many or as few as apply, and use them as jumping-off points to develop questions more suited to the students involved in the project.

Before Drama Workshops Begin

- What is drama?
- I like/don't like drama because . . .
- Learning about drama is important because . . .

During Drama Workshops

- Students evaluate themselves and their participation.

  When and why did you feel successful today/this week?

  When and why did you feel frustrated today/this week?

  How did the drama classes help you this week?

  What did you do in drama class this week that made you proud of yourself?

  What was the most important thing you learned this week that you never knew before?

- Students evaluate their contribution.

  How did your participation contribute to today's/this week's class(es)?

  What changes would you like to make for yourself tomorrow/next week?

  In what activities did you participate as a leader this week? What did you do that made you a leader? How did the other students in your group respond to you as a leader?

- Students evaluate the other members of their group/class.

   Who in your class made some important contributions in class this week? What did she do that you felt was important?

   How well did your group work together this week? What did the group do that you think was good?

   How did you solve problems if your group did not agree? Give an example.

   Did you ever compromise and give up what you wanted to do? How did that turn out?

   How can your group work better as a team? What can you do to help the group?

   How do you think drama class went this week? What did the class do that was successful? What did the class do that was not so successful? What could your class improve on?

- Students offer constructive criticism to each other.
- Students suggest ideas for continued exploration.
- Students describe what is hard about doing drama.

OUTLINE OF THE PROCESS

Facilitating Drama Activities

A Drama Instructor Should . . .

- be a guide, rather than a director;
- be an attentive audience member;
- be open-minded and nonjudgmental;
- be supportive, enthusiastic, and honest about students' discoveries and accomplishments;
- inspire within students the want for further exploration;
- pose questions without predetermined answers to stimulate discussion;
- be prepared to alter lesson plans when students suggest inspired ideas.

Tips for Facilitating Drama Sessions

- Attention should be complete. If the class is striving to be a supportive and working ensemble, it is important that everyone learn to listen to each other.

- Avoid asking students to "act." It does not really mean anything and suggests to them to "make it look fake." Instead, use phrases such as "Show me . . ."

- To facilitate exploration, ask questions about the characters, the characters' intentions, or the problems the characters are facing. Asking questions challenges students to find their own solutions. When students are given the chance to clarify their thoughts and intentions, they will discover more ideas to explore.

- Ask "What if?" This can be a very potent question. It helps open new areas of exploration. It is also a great way to offer suggestions without requiring them. The natural follow-up is "Why don't you try it?" and offering students another go at it.

- Praise students for what they have accomplished first, then offer new ideas and areas for exploration.

- Be precise about feedback, noting what worked well, what the students discovered, what else they might try, and what challenges they still face.

- If too much time is spent too early focusing on the exact words the students are saying, they will start contributing less, afraid of being wrong. When they contribute, be it one word or a full paragraph, they should be praised for their contributions. They will be encouraged to discover and contribute more.

- When sharing developing ideas or scenes, be sure each group gets a chance.

- If things go wrong, or off course, let the students try to fix it, most especially when groups are in the midst of a scene. Students should learn to work it out on their feet.

- If students giggle in the midst of creating a scene, it is usually a sign they are still uncomfortable with the particular activity or technique. It is often a part of the process. Give them the time to work past the uncomfortableness. Students cannot be expected to achieve everything all at once. As time passes, more can be expected of them, especially if regular postdiscussions are held. Students will uncover new ideas and goals to focus on and slowly become more comfortable with the activities and techniques.

- Any time small groups are working simultaneously, make sure to visit each group so they have someone to talk to and discuss ideas with as they build and develop their scenes.

- Open discussions to all students. Encourage them to offer feedback in the same way as you, from the positive to the challenging.

I think it was great when they . . .

I really liked . . .

I was surprised by . . .

I think it might be better if they . . .

I did not understand when . . .

- If students say the dreaded, "I don't know . . ." offer them playful possibilities such as:
  - A surprise that will pop up during the scene, such as, a sudden rain, the discovery of a lost object, or suddenly remembering an important piece of information.
  - Another character appearing that complicates the situation, such as, a little brother who wants to play, a "big kid" looking for trouble, or a friend desperate for help.

Warming Up to Drama

I was shy and nervous but all that drama gave me a little or a lot of confidence to say or do something in front of a class or audience. It made me more confident and to always try my best at all times.

—SIXTH GRADER, KALIHI

General Focus Techniques

A time will come when small groups of students will be working on creating their own scenes and short plays. When the groups are all working, talking, sharing, and discussing, the classroom becomes abuzz with noise. It is a good, creative noise, but sometimes regaining attention takes a little doing. The following techniques offer simple ways to regain attention without the instructor having to raise her voice.

Clapping to Attention

Instructor claps "One two-and three four." Students respond by clapping "One two." (The rhythm matches the "Shave and a haircut, two bits" ditty.) Instructor repeats the clap and response until students' focus is completely on the instructor.

Clap/Snap If You Hear Me

Instructor says, "Clap once if you hear me," then claps. Instructor says, "Clap twice if you hear me," then claps twice. Instructor continues until all students are repeating the claps.

Freeze

Instructor says, "Freeze," and students immediately stop, completely still, awaiting instructors cue to relax.

Warm-up Activities

Clap in Circle

Instructor and participants stand in a circle. Instructor passes a single clap around the circle. The clap should make its way around the circle in order. Students should be encouraged to listen to the emerging rhythm. Try this several times. First, students should be encouraged to see how quickly they can pass the clap around the circle, then how a rhythm can be sustained.

Next, a "pairs clap" is passed around the circle. The first and second person face each other and clap simultaneously. The second person then turns to the third, and they clap together. The third turns to the fourth and so on around the circle. The object is for the two claps to sound like one. This will be awkward at first, as the students discover how to communicate with their neighbor. Avoid letting students count or give verbal cues. Repeat this several times. As the group discovers a sustained rhythm, the goal of simultaneous clapping will become very easy.

Cross Across the Room If . . .

Participants form two lines facing each other. The instructor says "Cross across the room if . . ." completing the statement with some type of criteria ("you're wearing shorts," "have long hair," "like homework"). Students cross to the other line if the criteria fit. In this activity, students can "lie," crossing even if they do not fit the criteria. This ensures that no one is put on the spot, increasing the fun of the game. Give students a chance to call out the criteria as the activity progresses.

Walk About

Participants walk about the room, not touching anyone. Instructor calls out "Freeze" randomly. Students should come to an immediate stop, no matter what position they hold.

Instructor changes the direction of the walk, calling out "forward," "sideways," "backward." Students move accordingly. Instructor calls out parts of the room for students to focus on as they walk.

Instructor changes the style of the walk, calling out "slow," "quick," "big," "small," "lazy," "happy," "angry," "sad," "scared," "secretive," and so on. Instructor then combines different styles (slow and big, happy and quick).

Instructor plays a simple rhythm on a drum or the like, while students try to walk exactly to that rhythm.

Slow-Motion Race

Students line up in groups of five or six at one end of the room. The students "run" across the room as slowly as possible, in motion at all times. The slowest individual in each round "wins."

Wax Museum

Students spread themselves evenly about the room and freeze. As the instructor walks among them, students should move whenever the instructor is not facing them and freeze again when the instructor looks. If the instructor sees a student move, that student is out. Play until only one student is left.

This is an amazingly popular activity, which is good, because the activity is useful when attention has lagged and energy is low. This activity helps reenergize and refocus the group.

Mirrors

Students pair up. Pairs decide who is person A and who is person B. To start, person A is designated the leader and person B the mirror. Person B mirrors the movements of person A as if A is standing in front of a real mirror. Challenge the pairs to move in sync with each other, slowly and steadily, not trying to trick or throw off their partners. Students should work together closely, so an outside observer would have a hard time knowing who the leaders are. Encourage the leaders to explore movement with the whole body and different ways to move. After a designated amount of time, person B becomes the leader.

Statues

Students pair up. Pairs decide who is person A and who is person B. To start, person A is the leader and person B the statue. Person A molds person B into whatever he/she wishes. Person B must hold whatever pose into which they are sculpted. After a designated amount of time, persons A circulate the room and view the other statues. Person B then becomes the leader. As a variation, pick specific character types for the pairs to mold each other into. Encourage students to avoid telling each other how or what to move or demonstrating what they want their partner to do.

Once students have mastered working together, try this activity but without touching or without telling each other what or how to move.

The leaders place their hand just inches away from the part of person B they wish to move. Person B follows "magically" into the position person A is attempting to sculpt. Focus and concentration increase with the no-touching addition.

Student pairs then do the same, but standing at least ten feet apart from each other. Again, no talking or demonstrating.

Who's the Leader?

The class sits together in a circle. Instructor introduces the activity while leading simple, repetitive movements (slapping hands on knees, touching shoulders then head, clapping, knocking on the floor, and so on). The instructor encourages the students to mirror the movements. After the students have caught on to the premise of following the leader, a volunteer is sent out of the room. A second volunteer is chosen to be the movement leader. The movement leader begins the simple, repetitive movements with the rest of the class following. The first volunteer is brought back into the room and stands in the middle of the circle. That person must try to decide whom the movement leader is. The instructor challenges the sitting group to work together to avoid giving away the movement leader.

Change Three Things

Students pair up. Pairs decide who is person A and who is person B. To start, person A turns his back on person B. Person B changes three things about his appearance, and then person A turns back around and guesses what person B changed. Roles are then switched and the activity is repeated.

Ensemble-Building Activities

Spider Web

Students walk about the room, keeping themselves equidistant from each other so there are no big gaps between bodies. In Part One of this activity, the instructor calls out "Freeze" and all students freeze in place. In Part Two, the instructor says "stop" and all students look to see if there are big gaps between bodies. In Part Three, the instructor says "Stop" and any student that feels she should takes one step to spread out the bodies more evenly. In Part Four, the instructor calls "Spider web" and all students reach out to connect to as many others as they can while leaving one foot in place. Each part of this activity should be repeated more than once so the students can implement their understanding of each part.

Walking in Numbers

Students walk about the room, avoiding any physical contact. The instructor calls out a number. Students stick to each other in groups of that number. New numbers are called out periodically and all students regroup to match the new number. Any student not in a group is out. Any group not of the number called, either too small or large, is out as well. Play the game until only two students are left. Instructor will need to periodically remind groups to keep walking, as often they will stop in anticipation of the next number. By not stopping, students should be forced to not always group with friends.

Peas in a Pod

Participants take a walk about the room. As the instructor calls out specific criteria, students make groups according to the criteria. Criteria might include "What you ate for breakfast," "How many siblings you have," "Favorite flavor of ice cream," "The month of your birthday," "Color of your shirt." Set a time limit to achieve the goal (no more than ten seconds), and then go around the room asking each group what criteria they formed a group around and how they discovered each other. Begin with simple, obvious criteria (colors, hair length) and progress into more difficult criteria (birth month). As the activity progresses, provide communication challenges, such as using no words, sounds only, no words or sounds, using hands only, no hands, and so on.

Variations for this activity include groups attaching themselves to each other physically in an interesting formation, choosing a sound or word to represent themselves, or making a physical gesture to represent them.

Team Race

Students split into evenly numbered teams and line up in straight lines facing the instructor. The instructor calls out specific criteria (height, hair length, birth dates, shoe size). The teams line themselves up as quickly as possible, based on the criteria. When finished, team members place their hands on the shoulders of the person in front of them. The team that finishes first is checked for accuracy. If they succeeded, that team is awarded one point. The team that earns the most points wins.

Mappings

The instructor and students together imagine and discuss how a map of their community, town, city, state, nation, or the world is laid out in a large clear space. Once the map is clearly understood by everyone, the instructor asks students to place themselves on the part of the map that is, "Where you live," "Where your mother was born," "Where your mother's father was born," "Where that grandfather's parents were born," "Where you'd most like to visit," "Where you'd most like to live."

Developing Tools for Expression

The body and voice are communication tools and young people are the champions of expression, from shaking when they are angry to screaming when they are happy. However, their self-control does not necessarily mirror that accomplishment. In fact, learning to control and use their bodies and voices effectively to communicate ideas, specific actions, and events can be a challenge. They must practice focusing their energetic and expressive selves. In addition, as young people grow they become self-conscious, especially about their bodies.

Taking time to work out the embarrassment, encourage exploration and discovery and then turn their attention to focusing their newfound skills is an essential process. Do not rush it. If students are pushed too fast they will react in the opposite way. Their discomfort, embarrassment, and even fear will grow, becoming a defense against being forced into a process with which they still feel uncomfortable.

The following activities increase our comfortableness with using the body and voice as tools for expression and exercise our ability to be clear, concise, and focused. All these activities should be accompanied by discussions of effectiveness. As students learn to do it, they should also learn to see what is most effective. Students can offer feedback to each other and themselves and replay any action or scene to discover more and better ways to accomplish their task.

As will be seen in the sample drama lesson plans, each daily session emphasizes simple discussion, open-ended exploration, the building of experience through multiple attempts, and group self-evaluation. Over the course of the unit, their growing experience is gently put to practical application. In this manner students achieve some level of comfort, control, and focus, learn the questions they need to ask about using the skills, develop an eye for evaluating what works, and imagine these techniques for use in the devising sequence.

When introducing the tools for expression, it helps to start the discussion by asking the students what actors use to create characters. The answer probably will include costumes and the like. Do not ignore these answers; rather, gently guide the discussion to talk about what the actors (and all of us) use every day to express feelings, thoughts, and ideas. Build an understanding that the work they will do throughout the whole project, from the warm-ups in drama class to the final performances of the oral histories, begins with the imagination and is expressed through their voices and bodies. Without clear and precise use of their voices and bodies, all the costumes in the world will not make a difference. This is a very important point. Too often people turn to costumes, props, and set pieces far too quickly, impeding student creativity. The drama sessions are the time for exploration—the time to discover how the body and voice can be used to express a whole range of ideas, thoughts, characters, and meanings. Let this work be just that, exploration. Encourage students to find new and different ways each time an activity is done. If students ask for a prop or costume, ask them how else they might show how the character is using the prop or costume.

Imagination Warm-ups

Magic Box

With the class sitting in a circle, the instructor asks the students to imagine a box sitting in front of the instructor. The instructor then opens the box and takes out an object (a comb, mirror, toothbrush). The instructor demonstrates what the object is by the way he uses it. Students name the object. The instructor passes the box to a student, who pantomimes opening the box, removing an object, and using it. Students take turns opening and closing the box, demonstrating an object they remove.

Object Transformation

The instructor shows the class a simple object, like a chalkboard eraser. The instructor demonstrates the activity by transforming the eraser into something else (candy bar, walkie-talkie, telescope) by the way she uses it. Students name what the object has been transformed into. The object is then passed from student to student. Each transforms the object into something different. The other students guess.

Team Charades

Groups of five or six students line up, sitting on the floor. A single object is placed in front of each group. At a signal from the instructor, one member of the group at a time must transform the object into something else by the way he uses it. The other members of the group guess what the object has been transformed into. When someone in the group guesses correctly, the next member of the group transforms the object into something different from the first. The first group to successfully guess correctly what each member of their group has pantomimed scores a point. Switch objects among the groups. Ask students not to repeat their ideas from the first object.

Three Objects Become

Students break into small groups. Instructor hands each group three varied objects. The groups use the three objects in concert with each other to create a single idea. Students then act out the idea for the rest of the class. For example, a group is given a tennis racket, a cup, and a rope. The students create a boat ride, using the racket for a paddle, the cup for a telescope, and the rope for an anchor.

What Are You Doing?

In a circle, one student starts a simple action such as digging a hole. The next student asks, "What are you doing?" The first student answers with anything but what he is actually doing, such as brushing teeth. The second student must then start doing the named action (brushing teeth). Continue around the circle.

Creative Movement

Rhythm in Motion

Instructor establishes a set rhythm with a drum. Students walk to that beat.

Crazy Bodies

The class spreads itself evenly about the room, finding places to stand where no one will be touching each other or desks or the wall. On a cue from the instructor, students move their entire body without traveling. On a second cue from the instructor, students freeze. Instructor should encourage students to get every part of the body moving so each time they freeze, their body is in a completely different "crazy" position. Repeat, with students moving for three seconds, freezing, moving for three seconds, and so on.

Reduce the time to two seconds, then one, until students are freezing in "crazy" positions immediately on the cue of the instructor. Instructor encourages students to explore different levels and sizes (high, middle, low, big, little, tall, short).

Body Shaping

The instructor asks students for names of different kinds of shapes. The instructor then asks students to shape their entire body into different shapes on a count of five. As students create the shapes, the instructor encourages them to make the shapes in whatever way they wish, finding a way to get all parts of the body engaged. Shapes might include circle, square, triangle, rectangle, star, and diamond as well as twisted, curved, pointy, straight, crooked, angular, and so on.

After exploring realistic shapes, have the students explore "abstract shapes," such as lost, confused, sad, adventurous, a bad day, endless hunger, total happiness, secretive curiosity.

Group Shapes

Small groups work together as one to create the same shapes as above, starting with the realistic moving to the interpretive. The instructor should allow at least ten seconds for groups to accomplish the task.

Whole-Class Shape

The whole class works together as one to create the shapes as above, then to create a bowl of rice, a surfboard, a volcano, or other like ideas.

Vocal Exploration

"Oh"

Instructor asks students about the different ways people use the word *oh*. Everyone says "Oh" together. One student suggests an emotion or thought and everyone says "Oh" again, using the word to clearly express the suggested thought. Finally, one at a time students say the word again, using the word to express whatever emotion or thought they would like.

Soundscape

The instructor asks students to identify the kinds of sounds associated with a particular place or event (rain forest, city, football game, and so on). After a varied list has been developed, the instructor asks the students to each silently pick one of the sounds. On a cue from the instructor, all students simultaneously make the sounds, together creating a soundscape of the place or event. The instructor conducts by raising or lowering his hand to indicate different volume levels, and opening or closing his hand to indicate begin and stop. The class can work together to vary different sounds in a variety of ways to make the soundscape sound more like the real place or event. (For example, in a city the sound of a siren might start in the distance, get loud very quickly, and then disappear just as quickly.)

Body-Voice Combinations

Movement and Sound

Individual students create a household appliance through action and sound. Everyone practices simultaneously, then shares with the rest of the class.

Small groups of students work together to create a machine through action and sound. First, the groups create real machines (cars, planes, and so on), and then abstract machines with a purpose defined by the small group. After each, the small groups share with the rest of the class.

Small groups of students each create one of the following through a combination of action and sound: an amusement ride, a tropical storm on an island, a building blowing up, or a ship moving under a drawbridge.

Pantomime

Pantomime is a more advanced form of movement, focused on creating a reality where none truly exists. Although pantomime could easily be a part of the next section (Techniques for Devising), it is included here because it is an important tool in exercising and challenging students' physical abilities. Pantomime focuses students' attention on clarity and economy of movement, preparing them for the more difficult task of adding words later.

Sometimes the props used in a performance don't look very real because, due to lack of money or resources, some simple substitute had to be found or made. Sometimes the objects are imagined and pantomimed. The second solution is the more creative of the two and one to be encouraged in a project like this. By imagining or pantomiming the props, the whole process is made simpler (and possibly cheaper); more important, it challenges the students to be more focused, clear, and precise. Instead of having to worry about where their prop is or what they do with it while on stage, the students keep their focus on the character and the story. An example might be a dinner scene. Once plates, spoons, or cups are used, then it really becomes necessary to use actual food. Having food and liquid on stage for a two-minute scene is impractical, potentially messy, and scene stealing as the entire audience will be amazed that real food is being eaten and wonder how the young performers are able to speak and eat at the same time. When the audience is thinking about the food, the intent of the scene is lost.

When young people pantomime the needed objects, the audience is more focused on the participants.

Pantomime Activities

In the following activities, "who," "what," and "where" are used to indicate character, character intention, and location, respectively. "Want," indicates a character desire, a goal the character is trying to achieve.

Small-Group Action

Small groups either choose or are given a particular group action (crossing a river, hunting in the woods, spear fishing deep in the ocean, driving and getting on and riding a bus, building a snowman or sand castle, competing in a bike race, shopping in a clothing store, playing in the rain, planting a garden). Instructor challenges individuals within each group to find the variety of actions within the larger idea. Together the group creates a brief sequence showing the action. Each group shares with the rest of the class, who guess what the actions of the group and individual students are.

Small-Group "Where"

Small groups either choose or are given a particular place (playground, classroom, camp, kitchen). Instructor should be sure the place is somewhere many different people might be doing a variety of different actions. Each individual within the small group chooses a person and action of that place. Together the group pantomimes the place. Each group shares their scene with the rest of the class, who guess what the place is and what the actions of the individual students are.

Whole-Group "Where"

One volunteer moves to the center of the circle or in front of the rest of the class and performs an action that shows "where" they are and "who" they are in that place. When it is clear what the volunteer is doing, another student steps into that "where" but with a different "who." Continue, having others join in. The instructor encourages students to be aware of the setup of the "where," not walking through imagined doors, couches, tables, walls, and so on.

Small-Group Where/Who/What

Small groups choose a "where." Each student in the group takes on a role of a different character that might be at that "where." Each character should have a "want." The small groups act it out without speaking. (Example: A bus stop. A young boy, an older man, and an older woman. The older woman and young boy are sitting when the old man walks up. *Without* saying anything, the old man has to indicate he wants the seat. However, the boy wants to lie down on the seat. What does the old woman want?) Instructor encourages students to explore the reality of the situation, avoiding unrealistic solutions or interactions (such as violence or just running away).

Techniques for Devising

Tableaux

A tableau is a frozen image created by a small group of students, which communicates an idea or a single moment of action from a story or event. When done well, a tableau consists of strong actions suggesting what the characters are doing, how they are interacting with each other and the situation. A tableau should have a strong point of focus and consist of a variety of levels, actions, and character intentions.

Tableau is an underappreciated technique. Young people respond incredibly well to the clarity, ease, and effectiveness of creating still images. The technique provides just enough challenge to focus young imaginations on finding characters, specific actions, and activities for the characters, interrelationships with other characters, specific confines of the space the character inhabit, and the layout of the space before taking on the bigger challenge of building a fully fleshed out scene or short play. Tableaux . . .

- can be created quickly with a great deal of fun and burst of imagination;
- allow for simple feedback and quick reexploration;
- can help easily introduce a number of ideas: use of the body, character focus, character interaction, use of space, placement of bodies in space, sequence of action;
- offer rich, detailed, and easily accessible exploration that leads directly to a clear understanding of story sequence, an essential first step in transforming the story into a scene or short play;
- offer the possibility for clean and clear control by the young performers (if they create tableaux for both the beginning and ending of every scene, they have a mutually agreed upon starting and ending point with their fellow players);
- help clearly identify when scenes begin and end for an audience.

Tableau is a great way to have students simultaneously explore a story's sequence and prepare to develop the story into scenes or a short play. Without an understanding of the story's sequence, students get overwhelmed by deciding what to focus on as they build scenes or short plays. Starting with tableau helps them break the story into its essential pieces. Once they have created a series of tableaux illustrating the storyline, then they have also already chosen the parts to play, decided on the actions of the characters and how the characters are interacting with each other, and gotten a general sense of their own character's reactions and emotional responses to the action. They have also broken the story down into more manageable pieces to build into scenes.

Combining Tableaux with Narration

A narrative-tableau combination can be used in many ways. Aside from reinforcing students' understanding of the overall sequence of the story, it can also be used as a performance itself. Tableaux by themselves can be a simple and elegant statement about an idea. Think of the statue of Iwo Jima.

- A series of tableaux can become a slide show, watching the building of a story or event.
- A series of tableaux underscored by music can be powerful and very engaging performances.
- Narrated tableaux are simple ways to explore and present a story.
- Narrated tableaux offer the chance to explore things that might otherwise be difficult to stage (or to trust with highly energetic boys and girls): battles, surfing, car accidents, floods, bombing, fire, and the like.

Tableaux Activities

"Who," "what," and "where" are used to indicate character, character intention, and location, respectively. "Want" indicates a character desire, something the character hopes to achieve or the goal of the character.

Autoimages

The class stands in a circle. The instructor asks students to face outward, and then calls out a character or place. On the count of three, all the students turn inward, creating frozen images of the named character or place. Possible character types include a villain, hero, police officer, or teacher. Possible places include the beach, a doctor's office, or a bus stop. With each successive image, the instructor encourages greater exploration of levels, shapes, and clarity of action.

Spontaneous Group Tableaux

With students in small groups, the instructor calls out a particular place. The groups have ten seconds to create a tableau that suggests the named place. With each successive place, the instructor encourages the students to each find his own character and action within the tableau. The instructor also encourages groups to use a variety of levels. In an advanced form, the groups cannot communicate verbally as they create their tableaux.

Prepared Group Tableaux

Small groups are given a few minutes to plan, create, and practice a tableau based on a specific title given by the instructor. ("What's cool about your school?" "What's there to do in your community?" "What's unique about our culture?") The groups share their tableaux one at a time while others watch and interpret what they see.

Whole-Group Add-on Tableaux

The instructor asks for examples of a "where" such as a playground or beach. (Instructor should be sure the place is somewhere many different people might be doing a variety of different actions.) One student steps to the middle of the room and shapes his body to make an image of a character in that "where." Then, one at a time, other students add to the tableau with their own character and action. Participants should be encouraged to interconnect their images, suggestive of characters working together and/or in conflict with each other.

Tableaux/Thought-Track/Improvisation

(1) Small groups create a tableau based on a given theme such as "problems at school" or "being left out." (2) As the tableaux are shared, the instructor *thought-tracks* the characters: the instructor cues students one at a time by touching them on the shoulder. The cued student speaks a thought or line of dialogue aloud without moving from the tableau. (3) The tableau is then brought to life adding action and dialogue, but not necessarily the dialogue from the thought-tracking.

Improvisation

But I still can improve myself by letting loose a little more, add dialogue to my mini play and listen better to directions. I also realized that you should listen to other people's ideas as well as yours. Give other people a chance to talk.

—SIXTH GRADER, KANE'OHE

Improvisation is a technique for exploring and generating material for a scene or short play spontaneously. Participants create dialogue and action for their scenes or short plays, "making it up on the spot." With no prescripted dialogue or action, the participants are actively engaged during each practice or rehearsal session.

Improvisation is the core of this entire project. It needs no special equipment or space to work successfully. It offers participants the chance to contribute to their own level of comfort. It challenges them to become group players, working with and depending on each other to develop an effective, engaging, and pointed scene. It is a technique that also both frightens and excites. Many are afraid to dive into improvisation because there are no easy right answers. It requires participants to take risks with nothing but their imagination and intuition. For the facilitator, it requires great trust, allowing the participants to discover the skill, take the risk, and explore until understanding dawns.

Improvisation not only exercises participants' imagination and oral communication skills but also listening skills. As dialogue is not written down and memorized, young participants must actively respond and contribute to the ever-developing scene. With each rehearsal they not only understand the situation better and therefore develop a richer scene, they also come to realize the need for focus and listening. Without it, they will be lost and look foolish.

The most engaging aspect of improvisation is the opportunity to take full ownership of the process. When participants dive into improvisation, they generate every word, every idea, every action, and every move. The words they speak form into sentences that express ideas that, in the ideal situation, will speak to an audience. The participants capture the audience because they have taken complete control of the situation, both having created the scene or short play being presented and even improvising additional dialogue and action as the short play is in the midst of performance.

Improvisation often carries the preconceived notion that it is about comedy. Here, it is not. Improv comedy is a viable and vital form but not the style for exploring and staging oral histories. Participants revert to comedy during improvisations because comedy gets immediate reactions from an audience. To move beyond this, the participants should be well versed with information about characters and story (see the previous section on tableaux). They need to start with something that gives them a sense of where they are going with the improvised scene.

Exploring and Understanding Improvisation

Improvisation is the hardest skill for young people to accomplish. At first, either scenes are very short, devolve into meaningless comedy, or screech to a halt with students claiming "I don't know what else to say." The method many use to overcome this lack of skill and confidence is to write out the lines of dialogue. The instructor claims the students do not know what they are talking about or just cannot come up with good dialogue.

It is important that improvisation not be approached with the thought of finding the "right" or "most effective" dialogue. It should be about the participant expressing an understanding of an idea or situation. Dialogue does not just appear from nowhere. Dialogue needs to be connected to a goal, in theatre known as a character's intention. Once a participant in a scene has an idea of what his character is trying to achieve, then the improvisation has a firm foundation and a reason to be.

The second issue is comfort. No one gets better at something without repeated attempts. As young people try, their comfort level grows and their ability increases. This is why it is so very important for young people to explore these skills before using them to devise the oral history play from the oral history interviews.

Facilitating Improvisation

When students are first exploring ideas, let the improvisations run until they just stop or until the students find a way to bring it to some sort of conclusion. Interrupting improvisations, especially early ones, creates a sense of frustration and sets up the instructor as the only one who really knows when it is "right." Do not worry if what they are exploring is boring or will probably be thrown out. That's the process: To discover what works best, and what you want to keep, means you need to discover what you don't like as well.

Instructors can side-coach as improvisations are in action. This means gently encouraging students to stay focused on the action, on their character's intention, and to take risks to explore new ways to interact with the other characters to achieve their character's goal.

At the end of each practice, questions should be posed to the actors to encourage them to find more ways for their character to achieve their goals. Below is a short list of the types of questions that might be asked, but it is better if the students and instructor create their own list of questions from a developing class checklist of achievement. It is very important in the initial phase of exploring improvisation not to spend too much time evaluating the content of the scenes but to encourage further exploration. Content evaluation will set up an atmosphere of right/wrong stifling the kind of exploration that builds young people's confidence. It is also very important not to be bogged down with evaluating projection, enunciation, and the like. Focusing on these elements too early misplaces the focus of the exploration. Those techniques will be addressed later.

For the Participants

- How do you feel it went?
- Did you stay engaged throughout?
- Did you make strong choices?
- Did you build on the story or the character's intention?
- What moments were strong? What lines of dialogue? Actions?
- Which parts could be approached differently?
- Did your character give up on her intention? How else could your character take action to achieve that intention?
- How can you increase the urgency of the character's need to achieve?
- What actions can convey that urgency?
- How can your character use the information from the other character to help achieve his goal?

For the Viewers

- What parts of the scene were most interesting? Why?
- Where was it clear what the characters wanted? Where was it unclear?
- What other choices could the characters make to achieve their goal?
- Which parts were hard to understand?
- Finish these sentences:

  I think it was great when they . . .

  I really liked . . .

  I was surprised by . . .

  I think they might have done better if they had . . .

  I did not understand when . . .

Try to avoid adding too much "stuff" in the early explorations. Props and costumes should only be used when the students have explored and come to understand their short plays and scenes. Adding those elements too early puts too much focus on the objects, not the scenes.

Improvisation Activities

"Who," "what," and "where" are used to indicate character, character intention, and location, respectively. "Want" indicates a character desire, something the character hopes to achieve or the goal of the character. Initially focus the explorations on the "who" and "what." Once the students have demonstrated an understanding of improvisation, "where" can become a part of the action of the characters.

"Action" denotes two different ideas, the way the characters go about achieving their "what" or intention (setting up a meeting with another character, asking to extend curfew, bribing another character, impressing a potential date, passing lies) and the simple activities of the characters (setting the table, doing homework, digging in the garden).

"Yes, and . . ."

The whole group stands in a circle. The instructor begins by saying something like, "I went to the store." The students to the instructor's left says something like, "Yes, and I bought an ice cream cone." The next student says something like, "Yes, and I dropped the ice cream cone." This continues around the circle. The instructor encourages students to extend the activity with whatever comes to mind. Throughout the instructor should note how improvisation has two important principles: Speakers should not negate each other. (For example, "Give me back the dollar." "I didn't take your dollar." Such an exchange should be avoided. Instead say something like, "Give me back the dollar." "I'll give it back when you give me the baseball card you promised.") Speakers should never give just one-word answers.

The same activity can be done in small groups or pairs.

Spontaneous Dialogue

The instructor assigns pairs of students a "where" and "who." For example, (1) a student wants to copy another student's homework; (2) a parent confronts a child who comes home late from a friend's house. The pairs create a spontaneous dialogue appropriate to the assignment. The instructor encourages students to explore the "wants" of each character and how the characters actively get something from the other character in the scene. The instructor side-coaches students to avoid threats and bargaining. The instructor encourages the pairs to find active ways to obtain their goal.

Pair Dialogues

The instructor assigns pairs of students particular character objectives ("wants"). Pairs of students decide the "why" of the desire *before* starting, giving a focus to the improvisation.

- A bully is picking on a younger brother or sister. The older brother or sister confronts the bully.
- A child brings an animal home, trying to convince her mother to let her keep it.

- A teacher tries to teach the multiplication table to a student who only wants to talk about TV shows.
- A child desires to stay home from school and tries to convince her parent to stay home from work as well.
- A student tries to convince the teacher not to put an F on the report card, which comes out next week.
- One sibling tries to convince another who is shy to go to a party.
- Two friends are at a carnival. One wants to ride the newest roller coaster, and the other one is terrified to do so. He tries to convince the other not to ride without letting on that he is scared.
- The babysitter needs to get a child to go to bed. The child wants to stay up to (pick an activity), really because she is afraid of a monster.
- A friend wants to copy another friend's homework, but the second friend does not want to get in trouble.

Sharing and Building Stories

Children love stories. Children love playing out stories. Moreover, stories are powerful modes of communication that not only validate our own experience but also connect us to family, culture, and community. Sharing stories of our past helps us put our lives into perspective, making sense of who we are and what we can accomplish. By sharing stories of themselves and their family and creating original stories of their own, students not only gain a sense of self and their peers but also begin to discover how shared experiences bind us together as humans.

The sample drama lesson plans offer students the chance to collect and create their own stories while discovering what makes good stories. Students collect and share personal and family stories in an ongoing discussion of where and how to find stories while using drama techniques to imagine, create, develop, and perform an original story. These activities introduce the basic properties of a "good" story and expand literacy skills. The techniques can then be applied to explore and informally perform one (or more) of the shared personal/family stories.

Throughout, students should be encouraged to think about and discuss what makes effective and engaging stories. This will introduce them to the knowledge that all people, families, communities, and cultures have stories. Stories are not only found in books about faraway and strange places, but stories are living, ever-changing entities that help each of us understand more about our world, our culture, our community, our family, and, most importantly, ourselves. This will also slowly get them primed for the interview process. Having them first think about and share personal and family stories will help to get them thinking from the angle of the interviewee. Allowing them to ask questions about stories shared by the instructor, their peers, and family begins preparing them for the interview process.

When finally they work together to create and play out an original class story, they begin to see how they can shape these living stories into scenes and short plays in ways that both honor and enrich the story.

Sharing Personal Stories

When first starting to discuss and share stories, the instructor should share a story from her own childhood as a model and then ask students to share a memorable event from their own lives.

- Students bring to class special objects (or a picture of the object) connected to some important event in their life.
- Students pair up and interview each other about that object. (What is it? What do you do with it? Why is it important to you?)
- Each student shares the story of his special object.

The students will discover that objects often have meaning beyond their obvious use; they can be a way to understand more about a person or event and a way to find very particular, engaging stories. This also provides them with practice interviewing in a safe, informal environment. "Teaching students through their own experience is good pedagogy," the *Folk Life Standards* points out. "Students use this learning to examine something of interest to them—themselves—while building skills that are important throughout the curriculum: research skills, writing and speech skills, social skills, interpretive skills, and reflective skills."

Collecting and Sharing Family Stories

After experiencing stories from their own perspective, students should turn to family members to uncover memorable events about parents, grandparents, aunts and uncles, cousins, or whomever. Students should ask relatives to tell stories about their childhoods, particularly. The young always seem fascinated by the fact that adults were once children. Students should be encouraged to bring in photos, mementos, and artifacts that help illustrate the story they collect.

The students could also bring in stories from their particular culture or heritage. Sometimes older relatives are the keepers of traditional stories passed down by their relatives. For young people living in a country other than their ancestral home, this is an especially wonderful way to build a sense of connection to family and community.

When the students then retell these stories to the class, they have taken the next step in the oral history process—reviewing the essential sequence of the story they heard. As they learn to listen and retell, they are preparing themselves to reimagine the story dramatically.

Goal/Objectives

- to examine and understand how stories reflect who we are
- to explore how and where to find stories
- to introduce how a story can be "written" without paper and pen
- to explore the basic properties of a "good" story
- to inspire students to imagine and develop more detailed stories
- to demonstrate how depth of character and action can be enhanced using drama
- to make students more comfortable using the play-building techniques preparing them for creating scenes and short plays out of the oral histories
- to share stories of self, family, community, and culture

Creating and Developing an Original Story

Finally, as outlined in the sample drama lesson plans, students will learn ways to use the drama techniques to imagine, create, develop, and perform an original story. These activities expand students' literacy skills, both oral and written, by having students create stories though storytelling, develop the stories by playing them out, and, if desired, complete the process by writing their own version of the story. Through the process, students also discover and better understand the basic properties of a "good" story.

Basic Properties of a "Good" Story

- character
- want
- problem

Story-Building Activities

One-Word Story

The whole class works together to create an original story. Sitting in a circle, each participant contributes one word at a time. The words should connect to create sentences, and the sentences should string together to create a single story. When introducing this activity, explain that the story needs to make sense. For example, the following suggests two different stories, "Once an elephant was trotting down the street. A little girl fell in the mud." However, the following could be a single story, "Once upon a time an elephant was trotting down the street when a little girl saw him and was so scared she fell in the mud." Some guidelines to keep in mind throughout this activity:

- Students should not think too hard. It is only one word. Trust intuition.
- Words like *a, and,* and *the* are important words.
- Do not tell anyone else what word to say.
- If the story is hard to follow or not going anywhere, trash it and start anew. Keep in mind this is only an exploration. Starting a few different stories helps everyone get used to the idea. It is very hard to create a story only one word at a time.
- The whole point of this activity is to discover and make use of the most basic parts of a good story. The class should not try to create a complete story.

Group "Final" Story

In the final round of the one-word story activity, the class is challenged to incorporate all the properties of a good story. However, do not try to finish the story in the circle. Once the first problem the character encounters has been created, stop the story.

Small-Group Brainstorm

Each small group brainstorms one or two problems the character(s) of the story encounters trying to achieve his "want." Groups share their ideas.

Whole-Group Story Construction

The whole class works together to construct a "complete" story with a beginning, middle, and end incorporating as many of the brainstormed problems as possible. A resolution to the action will need to be decided by the class at this point.

Story Tableaux

The small groups create one or more frozen images of their assigned scene incorporating all members of the group.

Tableaux Storytell

The small groups develop a narrative to accompany their tableaux. Groups decide whether one person will narrate the tableau or whether all members of the group will share the narration.

Story in Dialogue and Action

Groups improvise dialogue and action for their assigned scene, developing fuller characters, more in-depth action, and a more fully explored series of events.

Sample Drama Lesson Plans

There are two sample lesson plans: a ten- and a fifteen-day plan. Drama instructors should reformat, lengthening or shortening the lesson plans, to focus on whatever skills are deemed necessary or useful for the participating students.

Materials

musical instruments (sticks, drum) for rhythm activities and clearly defining beginnings and ends of activities

a variety of simple, daily objects (tennis racket, funnel, handheld fan, cooking utensils, trays, cups, rope, paper plates, sports equipment)

chart paper and markers

Handouts

drama vocabulary

a family story data sheet

Visual Aids

drama vocabulary posters

Suggested Time Frame

Sessions are designed to last forty-five to sixty minutes.

What Are You Working Toward?

First, an atmosphere of fun should be built up around drama class. Students should have a good time. Enjoying themselves means students will look forward to class and the learning that accompanies it. This sense of fun should not be lost throughout the process. Allow time to play, returning to favorite activities and warm-ups. Keeping the class light, fun, and engaging keeps young people turned on about learning through and about drama and theatre.

Second, students should be "engaged in the moment." Students are looking for something to wrap their understanding around. As they are searching, they may be tentative about fully investing themselves in the drama task. By giving the students time to explore in order to understand the drama techniques (and eventually the oral history stories), they will both invest in the process and take control of it, gaining the confidence and knowledge needed to build and perform their scenes and short plays.

Steps in the Process

The following chart is a general guideline for tracking student progress in becoming comfortable with and applying drama skills. The chart should be seen as a way of finding out which students and/or groups need more help and time. In general, students will spend the greatest amount of devising and rehearsal time at levels two and three. The desire is they will have the time and get the support to reach level four. Please note that both levels three and four are stage worthy, meaning students could share the work with an audience. Substitute the words *tableau, pantomime,* or *short play* for the word *scene* as appropriate to the work the students are doing at any given moment.

This four-level scale breaks down as follows:

- One describes what the work might look like if students are unengaged in or uncomfortable with the process. These students need more attention and time.
- Two describes beginning-level work, meaning students are engaged in the work but not comfortable or skilled yet. These students need more time to explore, reflect, and improve on their skills and/or scenes.
- Three describes competent work. These students are making a scene work. With more time, they could be encouraged and challenged to move to level four.
- Four describes original and thoughtful work done by students excited by the process of exploration and creation, wanting to dive deep into the characters and story, searching for ideas and discoveries that not only they enjoy but will excite their audience.

The students should also help develop a list of their own based on their developing understanding of the drama skills. If students regularly share and evaluate their in-class work, they will become better at working with the techniques and should become better at identifying successful results and evaluating ineffective choices.

> *HTY [Honolulu Theatre for Youth] is a great thing that not only teaches you about acting it teaches you about life. I've learned that if you don't participate and you're shy you'll never get that shyness out of you. My voice to me has been harnessed and put to a good use.*

More over, I think that I am more committed to what I am doing unlike back in September, because I've learned to let myself go. One thing I can and will improve is my focusness. I need to work on not having any other side conversations and pay attention to what is going on. I also need to work being just a little more committed. I am holding back just a little bit. I got to learn to hang loose and have fun.
—SIXTH GRADER, KANEʻOHE

Level One

Participants

- are self-conscious, afraid of audience or fellow student reaction;
- focus on their own ideas;
- laugh, mumble, or direct others;
- create action primarily with their hands, their bodies giving no sense of character;
- falter with dialogue, or say nothing;
- cannot be heard.

A Scene

- is unclear, unfocused, and rushed;
- is static—there is no forward motion;
- lacks any sense of characters, setting, action, or events;
- lacks a central idea;
- is predictable and imitative;
- happens out of view of the audience.

Level Two

Participants

- are aware of the audience or other viewers and shy away from them;
- are aware of partners' contributions, but don't build on them;
- are unable to sustain focus, fading in and out during a scene;
- convey character action or intent using bodies, but with a lack of commitment;
- create dialogue and/or action that has little connection to characters, relationships, or events;

- speak clearly, but too softly;
- are unprepared for each new event within a scene.

A Scene

- is clear, but lacks emotion, purpose, or reason;
- stays focused on a single event, with little forward motion;
- offers some sense of character, setting, and event but with no emotional reality;
- has a beginning, but peters off;
- is predictable but built from the participants' own idea;
- has little purpose as it lacks goals for the characters;
- occasionally opens up to an audience.

Level Three

Participants

- are aware of the audience, creating scenes that can easily be seen and heard;
- work well together;
- sustain the scene, but are distracted by outside viewers and mistakes;
- clearly convey character action and intent through use of whole bodies and strong voices;
- generate dialogue that defines character purpose and intent, moving the story forward;
- can be heard, although they may be concentrating too heavily on just being loud;
- explore and expand on characters, events, and situations, both in planning and in execution.

A Scene

- is simple, but evocative of a central idea;
- moves from moment to moment in a logical sequence;
- contains clear characters, setting, and a sequence of events but with little emotional reality;
- has a clear beginning, but moves too quickly to an unsatisfying end;
- contains inventive ideas, with participants building on each other's contributions;

- contains conflict, but character action needs to be stronger and more urgent, with a particular goal;
- is clearly played for an audience.

Level Four

Participants

- communicate effectively with the audience;
- work well together, building on each other's contributions and ideas;
- are clearly focused, committed to the reality of the situations and story;
- clearly communicate character action and intent through a dynamic and imaginative blend of bodies and voices;
- develop and continue to improvise dialogue and action that evolve naturally from the objectives and conflict of the characters' situations;
- create characters with clear, strong objectives that are in conflict with each other;
- easily incorporate new information or events as they occur during the playing or performance of a scene.

A Scene

- is full of surprises and engaging ideas that reveal character action, intent, conflicts, and relationships;
- transitions smoothly from moment to moment, rising to a logical and satisfying conclusion;
- offers a clear and engaging sense of characters, setting, relationships, events, and emotional reality;
- has a definite beginning, middle, and end, each part building smoothly on the last;
- is an original and engaging exploration of a clear central idea;
- is built on strong and believable character actions that come into conflict with each other, ending with a satisfying resolution of the conflict;
- plays for and builds from the excitement of an audience.

Fifteen-Day Lesson Plan

Session One

A. Warm-up

Clapping in circle

B. Question of the day

"What are the skills we need to work successfully with others?"

C. Vocabulary for the day: "ensemble"

D. Ensemble activities

1. Peas in a pod

2. Walking in numbers

3. Spider web

4. Team race

E. Discussion

Introduction to the project

F. Journal reflection

How did your participation contribute to today's class? What changes would you like to make for yourself tomorrow?

Session Two

A. Question of the day

"How did we use ensemble yesterday?"

B. Warm-up

Cross across the room if . . .

C. Vocabulary for the day: "focus/listening"

D. Focus/listening activities

1. Who's the leader?

2. Change three things

3. Walk about

4. Rhythm in motion

E. Discussion

Project theme

F. Journal reflection

What was the word for today? How did we use it? What were examples of ensemble today?

Session Three

A. Warm-up

Object transformation

B. Questions of the day

"What is drama? What 'tools' do we use when doing drama?"

C. Vocabulary for the day: "imagination"

D. Imagination activities
  1. Team charades
  2. Three objects become

E. Discussion
  Collecting family stories

F. Journal reflection
  How well did your group work together? What did the group do that you think was good?

Session Four

A. Question of the day
  "With what 'tools' do we communicate in drama?"

B. Warm-up
  Mirrors

C. Vocabulary for the day: "body"

D. Body activities
  1. Crazy bodies
  2. Body shaping
  3. Group shapes
  4. Whole-class shape

E. Discussion
  Collecting family stories

F. Journal reflection
  When and why did you feel successful/frustrated today?

Session Five

A. Warm-up
  "Oh"

B. Questions of the day
  "What is a story? What makes a good story?"

C. Vocabulary for the day: "voice"
  Vocal exploration
  Soundscape

E. Body/voice combinations
  Movement and sound

F. Journal reflection

What did you do in drama class this week that made you proud of yourself?

What was the most important thing you learned this week that you never knew before?

Session Six

A. Warm-up

Wax museum

B. Question of the day

"How are stories communicated?"

C. Activities

1. One-word story.

2. Basic properties of a "good" story are introduced.

3. Group incorporates the properties as the activity continues.

D. Journal reflection

How are you feeling about this class? What's good? What's not? What could we improve on? How?

Session Seven

A. Warm-up

Statues

B. Questions of the day

"What are stories you like? Movies? Books? Plays? Oral tales?"

C. Vocabulary for the day: "tableau"

D. Tableau activities (in small groups)

Spontaneous group tableaux

E. Story activities

1. Group "final" story

2. Small-group brainstorm

3. Whole-group story construction

F. Group discussion

"What makes our story interesting? Why?"

G. Journal reflection

How have you made important contributions in drama class? What did you do that you felt was important?

Session Eight

A. Questions of the day

"Who has stories? Who can you ask for a story?"

B. Warm-up

Autoimages (using characters and images from the class story)

C. Vocabulary for the day: "tableau"

D. Discussion

"What makes a good tableau?"

E. Story-building activities

1. Divide the story into sections that match the number of small groups.

2. Assign one section to each small group.

3. Story tableaux:

   a. Groups share their tableaux in story order.

   b. Groups comment on effectiveness and possible suggestions for further exploration.

   c. Groups reexplore and reshape their tableaux.

   d. Groups share their tableaux in story order.

F. Journal reflection

How well does your group work together? What did the group do that you think was good?

How do you solve problems if your group did not agree? Give an example.

Session Nine

A. Questions of the day

"What are the key vocabulary words we've been exploring? Give an example of how we've used them."

B. Warm-up

Quick review of yesterday's tableaux

C. Vocabulary for the day: "narration"

D. Story-building activities

1. Tableaux storytell.

2. Groups practice storytelling and tableaux together.

3. Groups share their storytelling/tableaux in story order.

4. Groups discuss the storytelling/tableaux, commenting on effectiveness and possible suggestions for further exploration.

E. Journal reflection

What have you done in drama class that has made you proud of yourself?

Session Ten

A. Question of the day

"Who has a family story to share?" (Volunteer shares a story.)

B. Warm-up

What are you doing?

C. Vocabulary for the day: "pantomime"

D. Pantomime activity

Small-group "where"

E. Story-building activities

1. Groups reexplore their narrated tableaux.

2. Groups share their storytelling/tableaux in story order.

F. Journal reflection

How do you think drama class went this week? What did the class do that was successful? What did the class do that was not so successful? What could your class improve on?

Session Eleven

A. Question of the day

"Who has a story to share?" (Volunteer shares a story.)

B. Warm-up

"Yes and . . ."

C. Vocabulary for the day: "improvisation"

D. Story-building activities

1. Story in dialogue and action.

2. Groups practice their developing scene.

3. Groups share their scenes in story order.

4. Groups discuss the various scenes, commenting on effectiveness and possible suggestions for further exploration.

E. Journal reflection

In what activities have you participated as a leader? What did you do that made you a leader? How did the other students in your group respond to you as a leader?

Session Twelve

A. Question of the day

"Who has a story to share?" (Volunteer shares a story.)

B. Warm-up

Spontaneous dialogue/pairs dialogue

C. Vocabulary for the day: "improvisation"

D. Story-building activities

1. Each group is given a chance to reexplore and reshape their scene.

2. Groups present their scenes in a final sharing of the complete story.

E. Group discussion

"How can we use what we've learned to develop our own plays?"

F. Journal reflection

Who in your class has made important contributions in class? What did she do that you felt was important?

Session Thirteen

A. Question of the day

"How can we use what we've explored to create a play from a story?"

B. Discussion of in-class stories

C. Warm-up

Mappings

D. Individuals share personal or family stories with their small group

1. The group chooses one story.

2. The group breaks down the story into scenes.

E. Journal reflection

What is the most important thing you have learned in drama class that you never knew before?

Session Fourteen

A. Warm-up

Class favorite

B. Group tableaux for the scenes of their story

1. Groups share their tableaux in story order.

2. Groups comment on effectiveness and possible suggestions for further exploration.

3. Groups reexplore and reshape their tableaux.

4. Groups share their tableaux in story order.

C. Group storytelling/tableaux sequence

1. Groups practice storytelling and tableaux together.

2. Groups share their storytelling/tableaux in story order.

3. Groups discuss the storytelling/tableaux, commenting on effectiveness and possible suggestions for further exploration.

D. Journal reflection

How can your group work better as team? What can you do to help the group?

How has drama class helped you?

Session Fifteen

A. Warm-up

Class favorite

B. Group reexploration of their story in dialogue and action

1. Groups share their stories.

2. Groups discuss the various stories commenting on effectiveness and possible suggestions for further exploration.

3. Groups reexplore and reshape their stories.

4. Groups share their stories.

C. Journal reflection

Learning about drama is important because . . .

Ten-Day Lesson Plan

Session One

A. Warm-up

Clapping in circle

B. Question of the day

"What are the skills we need to work successfully with others?"

C. Vocabulary for the day: "ensemble"

D. Ensemble activities

1. Walking in numbers

2. Spider web

3. Team race

E. Vocabulary for the day: "focus/listening"

F. Focus/listening activities
   1. Walk about
   2. Rhythm in motion
G. Discussion
   Introduction to the project
H. Journal reflection
   How did your participation contribute to today's class? What changes would you like to make for yourself tomorrow?

Session Two

A. Warm-up
   Object transformation
B. Questions of the day
   "What is drama? What 'tools' do we use when doing drama?"
C. Vocabulary for the day: "imagination"
D. Imagination activities
   1. Team charades
   2. Three objects become
E. Discussion
   Project theme
F. Journal reflection
   How well did your group work together? What did the group do that you think was good?

Session Three

A. Question of the day
   "What 'tools' do we use to communicate in drama?"
B. Warm-up
   Mirrors
C. Vocabulary for the day: "body"
D. Body activities
   1. Crazy bodies
   2. Body shaping
   3. Group shapes
E. Vocabulary for the day: "voice"
F. Vocal exploration
   Soundscape

Figure 2–2.
Student journal entry showing an example of tableau

G. Body/voice combinations
   Movement and sound
H. Discussion
   Collecting family stories
I. Journal reflection
   When and why did you feel successful/frustrated today?

Session Four

A. Warm-up
   Statues
B. Questions of the day
   "What is a story? What makes a good story? What are stories you like? Movies? Books? Plays? Oral tales?"
C. Activities
   1. One-word story
   2. Basic properties of a "good" story
   3. Incorporation of the properties as the activity continues
D. Vocabulary for the day: "tableau"
E. Tableau activities (in small groups)
   Spontaneous group tableaux
F. Story activities
   1. Group "final" story

    2. Small-group brainstorm

    3. Whole-group story construction

  G. Group discussion

    "What makes our story interesting? Why?"

  H. Journal reflection

    How have you made important contributions in drama class? What did you do that you felt was important?

Session Five

  A. Questions of the day

    "Who has stories? Whom can you ask for a story?"

  B. Warm-up

    Autoimages (using characters and images from the class story)

  C. Vocabulary for the day: "tableau"

  D. Discussion

    "What makes a good tableau?"

  E. Story-building activities

    1. Divide the story into sections that match the number of small groups.

    2. Assign one section to each small group.

  F. Story tableaux

    1. Groups share their tableaux in story order.

    2. Groups comment on effectiveness and possible suggestions for further exploration.

    3. Groups reexplore and reshape their tableaux.

    4. Groups share their tableaux in story order.

  G. Journal reflection

    How well does your group work together? What did the group do that you think was good? How did you solve problems if your group did not agree? Give an example.

Session Six

  A. Questions of the day

    "What are the key vocabulary words we've been exploring? Give an example of how we've used them."

  B. Warm-up

    Quick review of yesterday's tableaux

  C. Vocabulary for the day: "narration"

D. Story-building activities
   1. Tableaux storytell.
   2. Groups practice storytelling and tableaux together.
   3. Groups share their storytelling/tableaux in story order.
   4. Groups discuss the storytelling/tableaux, commenting on effectiveness and possible suggestions for further exploration.
E. Journal reflection
   What have you done in drama class that has made you proud of yourself?

Session Seven

A. Question of the day
   "Who has a family story to share?" (Volunteer shares a story.)
B. Warm-up
   What are you doing?
C. Vocabulary for the day: "pantomime"
D. Pantomime activity
   Small-group "where"
E. Story-building activities
   1. Groups reexplore their narrated tableaux
   2. Groups share their storytelling/tableaux in story order
F. Journal reflection
   How do you think drama class went this week? What did the class do that was successful? What did the class do that was not so successful? What could your class improve on?

Session Eight

A. Question of the day
   "Who has a story to share?" (Volunteer shares a story.)
B. Warm-up
   "Yes and . . ."
C. Vocabulary for the day: "improvisation"
D. Story-building activities
   1. Story in dialogue and action.
   2. Groups practice their developing scene.
   3. Groups share their scenes in story order.
   4. Groups discuss the various scenes, commenting on effectiveness and possible suggestions for further exploration.

E. Group discussion

"How can we use what we've learned to develop our own plays?"

F. Journal reflection

In what activities have you participated as a leader? What did you do that made you a leader? How did the other students in your group respond to you as a leader?

Session Nine

A. Question of the day

"How can we use what we've explored to create a play from a story?"

B. Discuss in-class stories

C. Warm-up

Mappings

D. Sharing of individuals' personal or family stories with their small group

1. The group chooses one story.

2. The group breaks down the story into scenes.

E. Journal reflection

What is the most important thing you have learned in drama class that you never knew before?

Session Ten

A. Warm-up

Class favorite

B. Group-created tableaux for the scenes of their story

1. Groups share their tableaux in story order.

2. Groups comment on effectiveness and possible suggestions for further exploration.

3. Groups reexplore and reshape their tableaux.

4. Groups share their tableaux in story order.

C. Group-created storytelling/tableaux sequence

1. Groups practice storytelling and tableaux together.

2. Groups share their storytelling/tableaux in story order.

3. Groups discuss the storytelling/tableaux, commenting on effectiveness and possible suggestions for further exploration.

D. Journal reflection

How can your group work better as a team? What can you do to help the group? How has drama class helped you? Learning about drama is important because . . .

3

Interview Skill-Building

I hope I get to talk like this to my grandma before she passes away and I regret that I didn't get to talk to her.
—Sixth grader, Wahiawa

At a Glance

Students experiment with, explore, and discuss how to develop questions and conduct effective interviews by conducting mock interviews with fellow students and teacher(s).

Goals/Objectives

- to prepare students to conduct oral history interviews
- to introduce the basic properties of conducting a good interview
- to introduce students to the basics of creating effective questions
- to introduce students to the idea of listening to answers to get more answers
- to enhance students' oral and written communication skills

61

Interview Lessons

Interviews bridge communities, making this whole project personal and unique. Through the interview process, students share in the world of the informant, becoming a part of it and investing themselves in it, making the interviews a very active form of learning. The interviews can also be a wonderful exploration or even introduction to some of the students' own family history and culture or their community.

However, the interview process is a challenging one for students not skilled in asking questions. Our experience showed that the vast majority were unskilled not only at asking probing questions but also at developing follow-up questions. At first, students created a series of questions they obediently wrote down, but then we found they slavishly stuck to only those questions.

Q: Where did you grow up in Wahiawa?

A: I didn't grow up in Wahiawa, I grew up in Helemano.

Q: Did you like growing up in Wahiawa?

A: Do you mean Helemano? Because I didn't grow up in Wahiawa.

We created a series of interview lessons to help the students understand the philosophy of creating and conducting an interview. Although the workshop helped some, this was one of the hardest parts of our work. Much experimentation went into the development of these lessons.

The resulting work has been well received by teachers because developing and asking questions is a useful skill in many subject areas. Investigations, inquiry, and research all require knowledge of how to ask effective questions and how to reach the heart of an issue.

The first rule of conducting interviews in preparation for a dramatic experience is: Interviews are about finding a fascinating story or sequence of events, not about collecting facts. All too often when conducting interviews, students collect facts. Their questions consist of "How old were you when. . . ?" and "How much did it cost for. . . ?" and "Did you have. . . ?" These questions, while interesting, will not provide significant material for a drama-based project. Students need time to experiment with creating, asking, and following up on questions.

Up to this point in the process, students have informally used interviewing techniques to collect and tease out stories. Now the process of asking questions and conducting an interview becomes the focus. Young people's ability to conduct interviews and ask effective questions increases with practice. At first, most will not know how to develop questions or even what questions they should be asking. If this is the first time the students will be creating questions and conducting formal interviews, their initial suggestions for questions will often be short. Through a series of lesson plans focused on discussions about questions and interviews and participating in mock interviews, the students will become more comfortable and proficient at asking questions. During these lessons, the students should understand all of the following.

- All questions are welcome.
- No one should make fun of a question.
- Questions should come from their own special interests.
- Spontaneous questions during an interview are welcomed.

Students will become caught up in the questioning and interviewing when they have an interest in the theme or topic. If the theme or list of topics the class creates is too narrow, or prescribed by the teacher, the students will be less likely to get involved. When creating a list of topics within the project theme, all students should contribute, just as they will all participate in the interview itself.

Listening, Questioning, and Following Up

The parallel challenge is how well students actually listen to the answers. Our experience showed students often repeat a question already asked, sometimes immediately following the first. Teaching students to listen is a difficult process. We discovered that it was important to encourage them to have a goal, something particular to be listening for.

Our first attempt relied heavily on the students asking follow-up questions to learn more about a story. That met with limited success. Often the students heard the informant tell a "story," such as "The tofu factory I worked in burned down. A fire started in one of the pots and we had to close the factory for a year," and felt they had heard the whole story.

The next attempt consisted of challenging the students to find "golden moments," stories or pieces of stories they found most interesting. Having them write down just the golden moments as opposed to transcribing the whole interview helped focus their attention. They could choose when to listen closely and when not to, giving them a little self-chosen break during the interview. This worked a little better because then we could challenge the students to ask more questions based on their golden moment.

Finally, by sharing a list of topics with the students particular to the informant, the students could choose ahead of time what topics they were most interested in and create questions particular to that topic. Therefore, students concentrated on interviewing during their chosen topic and listening when other students were interviewing. It also gave the teacher the opportunity to work with one student or group at a time, exploring each topic to its fullest before moving on to the next.

For students to get the most out of an interview, they must practice. Giving young people the chance to conduct interviews with more than one person and more than once with the informant increases the chances that engaging and detailed material will be discovered.

JOURNAL RESPONSE QUESTIONS

A list of potential questions follows. This list was developed over time and with students in Hawai'i. Use as many or as few as apply and use them as jumping-off points to develop questions more suited to the students involved in the project.

Before the Interview Skills Workshop

- What is an "oral history interview"?
- In an interview I will learn about . . .
- I like/don't like talking with people because . . .
- Asking questions is important because . . .

After the Interview Skills Workshop

- How do you think the interview skills workshop went? What did the class do that was successful? What did the class do that was not so successful? What could your class improve on?
- Describe what is hard about this part of the process.
- What was the most important thing you learned that you never knew before?
- How did your participation contribute to this workshop?
- When and why did you feel successful?
- When and why did you feel frustrated?
- What did you do in the interview skills workshop that made you proud of yourself?
- What did you learn in the interview workshop that will help you with the real interview?

Preparing for the Interviews

- What are the most important ideas you should remember when conducting an interview?
- How are you feeling about conducting the interview? What do you think will happen? How can you best prepare yourself?
- When I am conducting the interview, I hope that . . .

OUTLINE OF THE PROCESS

Learning to Listen

Learning to listen will help students immensely in preparation for conducting the oral history interviews. Interviewers learn a great deal more by listening than by trying to ask all the questions on their paper. Moreover, between the isolated time of staring at televisions, handheld video games, and computers, and the almost nonstop conversation that young people seem to engage in constantly, students need time to exercise their listening skills.

Following are a few exercises focused on listening. As the class explores each, the drama instructor should watch to see how concentrated each student is and how much each recalls when the exercise is finished. Discuss with students how to tell if someone is listening. Is squirming in a chair listening? Where are a person's eyes focused when they are listening? When a person is finished listening, what should they be able to do?

Listening Exercises

- Challenge the class to stay quiet for as long as possible. When this is first tried, students may not be comfortable with the silence. Some will giggle or make little swallowing or grumbling sounds. Start over as many times as it takes until the class seems to be working together to achieve a significant time of silence. If this becomes a daily activity with the class challenging itself to beat its own time, students will learn to be at ease with silence, and may even learn to like it.
- Have students listen carefully for a set amount of time to all the sounds of a particular place, making a list of the sounds they hear.
- Play a musical recording. Ask students to . . .
  listen for particular instruments
  recall the lyrics
  draw a picture of what their imagination conjured up as they listened.

- When stories are shared during the drama lessons, take a few moments after each to have the students write down everything they remember about the story under a strict time limit (thirty to sixty seconds). Encourage them to make a list of words and phrases, not worrying about writing out the whole story.
- Read a story aloud, with the same follow-up.

Learning to Question

Today in drama class we talked to our teacher Mrs. "A" like she was a new person and a different person. So Dan gave us markers and a piece of paper and we started to write questions that we were going to tell Mrs. "A." She said I asked a very good and hard question. It was "When you were little what was your hardest challenge?"

—FOURTH GRADER, KALIHI

When students write down too many questions ahead of time, they stick to those questions no matter what the answers are. The difficult part of interview preparation is getting students not only to understand what makes good questions but also to create follow-up questions when they hear an interesting or dramatic story during the interview. The making good questions handout (see Appendix M, p. 162) is a guide to help students not only develop good questions but also remind them of the importance of asking follow-up questions on the spot.

Discuss the project theme when developing questions for the interview. This will help focus the interview and keep students from overwhelming the informant with too many unrelated questions.

Brainstorming

When discussing the theme, students should be given the chance to brainstorm words, phrases, and images based on that theme in preparation for developing specific topics and questions.

- In small groups, students are given markers and chart paper. The drama instructor asks the students to write or draw anything that comes to mind about the theme.
- After working for a short while, the drama instructor asks individual students to read some of the ideas they wrote down.
- The drama instructor then chooses a few of the ideas and students continue brainstorming from the new suggestions.

Preparing Questions

- Create smaller topics within the theme so small groups of students can focus on particular areas.
  - Ask, "What would you like to know about (the oral history informant)?"
  - Record the answers on a chart. Topics might include:

    Home life as a child —The house and land itself; household chores

    Child life —Favorite hero when growing up; person who had the biggest influence; biggest triumph in life; biggest challenge growing up; most embarrassing moment growing up; hardest thing you ever had to do; what was scary as a child?

    Memories of daily life as a child —Bathing and grooming; clothing, the fashions; best friends

    Memories of parents —Mother's work; Father's work; special memory of Dad, Mom, and brothers and sisters

    Memories of grandparents —Special memory of grandparents

    School days —Transportation to school; studies and homework; discipline; games and special school events

    Leisure activities as a child —Favorite games or sports; favorite toys; family trips and travel; swimming spots; favorite beaches, picnics, camping; holidays and/or community celebrations; family vacation spots

    Adult life—Work in the community; changes seen in the community; the affects of these changes on self, family, and the community

    Wars and wartime —Relatives who fought; patriotic events; memories of Pearl Harbor, D-Day, VJ Day; effects of the war on family and self
  - Review the list to develop questions out of the suggested ideas.
  - After creating the list, ask . . .

    "Which questions are going to get a yes/no answer?"

    "Which seems to get only one or two words for an answer?"

- Discuss questions:
  - What are the different ways to formulate questions?
  - What kinds of questions are about details? Which are about bigger issues?
  - How can we ask questions so that we can learn details?
  - How can we be more sensitive when we ask questions?

- Discuss what makes good questions using the making good questions handout.
  - Avoid close-ended questions (questions that get a yes or no answer).
  - Avoid "leading" questions, which encourage the informant to answer in a way that agrees with what you think rather than what he thinks.
  - Encourage the development of open-ended questions, using the five "W's" ("who," "what," "when," "where," "why") and "how."
  - Discuss the kinds of questions that might elicit answers connected to the theme/topic:

    What was the biggest challenge you faced when you were young?

    What was your happiest moment when you were young?

    What do you remember being sad about when you were young?

    What did you feel was your biggest triumph when you were young?
  - Encourage the use of "Tell me about the most _____ event that happened to you."
  - Be prepared with follow-up questions.

    Can you give me an example of that?

    Can you describe that in more detail?

    How did you feel about . . . ?

    What happened next?

    Who was there with you?

    How did she feel?
- Create a series of interview guide cards related to the theme, the topics, and the questions that might be asked (an example can be found in the Appendices):
  - Label each card at the top with the project theme and a single topic under the theme.
  - Develop a list of questions that address the particular topic on the card.
  - Label a section on each card "follow-up questions" and "golden moments."

    Leave the follow-up questions section blank. These will be developed during the interview, questions that will help find out more about interesting subjects or stories the oral history informant mentions. Questions like: Who was there? What happened before that? What happened next? Where did this take place? How long did it last? What did you learn from this? What was hard about it? Fun about it?

    Leave the golden moments section blank.

Learning to Conduct Interviews

- Ask students what should happen in a good interview. Record their answers on the board or on chart paper, then use those answers to help create a list of important points to remember. Hopefully, the list will include the following.
  - Be a good listener.
  - Ask questions in a way that gets people to talk about subjects that interest you.
  - Give the interviewee time to pause, think, and reflect.
  - Take time.
  - Relax and enjoy the interview.
- Discuss the need for being sensitive to the informant's feelings.
  - Personal questions should be asked only if the informant seems comfortable talking about very personal memories.
- Discuss the need to stay on the chosen topics.
  - If students are tossing out questions unrelated to the experience of the informant, guide them back to the topic.
- Discuss full-class participation.
  - Time should be allowed for everyone to ask questions.
  - If someone stumbles on a question or forgets it, it is all right to pass for the moment. That student can think about the question and ask again later in the interview.
  - If a student needs help, the teacher will offer assistance in stating a question.
- Discuss using the interview guide cards.
  - Be ready to pull out any of them at any moment depending on how the interview is proceeding.
  - Be ready also to stop using an index card if there are no answers for that topic. (For example, if your informant said, "I didn't have any chores," then no more questions need to be asked on that subject.)
  - Be ready to make notes on follow-up questions, golden moments, and stories or events of interest.

Sample Interview Skills Lesson Plan

Drama instructors should reformat, lengthening or shortening the lesson plan, to focus on whatever skills are deemed necessary or useful for the participating students.

Materials

paper, chart paper, pencils/pens/markers

Handouts

making good questions poster

interview guide cards

Suggested Time Frame

three sessions of forty-five to sixty minutes

What Are You Working Toward?

- Students actively engaged in asking probing, open-ended questions, forming follow-up questions that elicit golden moments or moments that suggest dramatic stories
- After the interview, an interview guide card filled with stories they found most fascinating

Interview Skills Lesson Plan

Session One: What Makes a Good Question?

A. Warm-up
  1. Autoimages
     a. You in drama class
     b. Personal feeling about drama
B. Brief introduction to this phase of the project
C. Finding a story about school
  1. In pairs, students find an interesting story about school from each other
  2. Partners retell the story to each other
D. Ask "What makes good questions?" Discuss briefly
E. Interview three students about bicycle riding
  1. Ask one student a "Did . . ." question. Note the length of the answer.
  2. Ask another student a "How/What/Why . . ." question. Note the length of the answer.
  3. Ask the third student a "Tell me about . . ." question. Note the length of the answer.

    4. Discuss the differences with the class and ask which question seemed strongest or elicited the fullest answer.

F. Discussion of questions and making good questions poster

    1. What makes effective questions? Discuss.

       a. Introduce the concepts of:

          i. Who/what/where/when/how;

          ii. Follow-up—"What happened next/before?"

          iii. Searching for a story—"Tell me a story about your most (surprising, sad tragic, mysterious, happy) memory."

G. Finding a story about the beach

    1. Two sets of partners

       a. One person interviews another to find an interesting story about the beach.

       b. Two members of the group listen, noting questions that are asked.

    2. Group writing

       a. Write down the questions that were asked.

       b. Make note of the most effective questions.

H. Journal reflection

Session Two: What Do We Ask Questions About?

A. Warm-up

In small groups, students have two minutes to list everything they learned yesterday about making good questions.

B. Drama instructor conducts an interview with another teacher, volunteer parent, or other adult.

Stop to note good and bad questions and how they relate to answers.

C. Drama instructor makes a list of topics about his life. Students choose one of the topics.

D. Small groups brainstorm questions for that topic and record them on chart paper.

E. Students ask questions of the drama instructor. Review good questions as necessary.

F. Evaluate the process

    1. Which were the most effective questions? Why?

    2. What did you discover in the short interview that was most interesting?

   G. Develop follow-up questions for the interesting stories.

   H. Ask follow-up questions.

   I. Journal reflection

Session Three: How Do We Conduct an Interview?

   A. Warm-up

   B. Review concepts

     1. "What makes a good question?"

     2. "What are the three parts of an interview?"

       a. Good questions

       b. Follow-up questions

       c. Finding golden moments

   C. Introduce interview guide cards

   D. Develop interview guide cards on drama instructor's topics (from day two).

     1. Small groups each pick one topic.

     2. Briefly discuss follow-up questions and golden moments.

   E. Class conducts interview with the drama instructor.

     1. Ask questions.

     2. Develop follow-up questions during the interview.

     3. Capture golden moments—anyone can, at any time.

   F. Debrief the process

   G. Prepare for the real interview

     1. Distribute new interview guide cards.

     2. Discuss basic information about the oral history informant.

     3. Pick out possible topics based on the shared information.

   H. Journal reflection

Examples of Drama Instructor Topics

- learning to ride a bike
- first trip on a railroad train
- adopting a brother
- catching my first fish
- snow sledding accident
- playing on the train tracks
- lost on the mountain
- the unlucky canoe trip

4

Collecting Oral Histories

I really think this is a great thing that we are learning about Wahiawa by interviews and not so much of just reading about Wahiawa.
                                                    —SIXTH GRADER, WAHIAWA

AT A GLANCE

Students conduct interviews with and record oral histories of family members, relatives, neighbors, or community members to find engaging and unique stories about their own community or family heritage.

GOALS/OBJECTIVES

- to collect oral histories of the community and family
- to stretch students' understanding of their community and family
- to offer students the chance to see the community as a place of learning
- to involve the community in the education of its young people
- to build connections between generations
- to uncover human stories within oral histories
- to record and preserve unique stories of the community

Preparing and Conducting Interviews

Initially, in the Honolulu Theatre for Youth (HTY) project, we sent students out to conduct interviews with grandparents, aunts, neighbors, or other community people. The students gathered incredible material, but the process proved very difficult to control and monitor. Would the students write down the information or record it? If they recorded it, who provided the equipment? Once recorded, who was responsible for the daunting task of transcribing? In addition, the students had little patience for taking notes, asking follow-up questions, or truly listening to the answers they were given. Unfortunately, these questions and observations arose only after we conducted the project the first time.

Another factor that necessitated a change was deciding on which stories to develop into the performance. With twenty-five students each having conducted a thirty- to forty-five-minute interview, there was far more interview material than we could ever use. This meant some of the students' work would not be validated.

After experimentation, we discovered that bringing the informants into the classroom and videotaping an all-class interview proved far richer. The students could concentrate on the questions and not the process of recording the answers. In addition, the stories became common property of all the students.

Spending time arranging, coordinating, and preparing for the interviews is a very important part of carrying off a successful project. The informants need the time to prepare, as many are nervous about speaking to a class of children. The students, too, need time to focus their questions and the interview.

We eventually expanded the process to two steps. The teacher conducts the first interview with the chosen informant by herself, accomplishing several goals. First, the informant is introduced in an informal way to the project and the process. Second, the teacher develops a working relationship with the informant. Third, the teacher develops a list of topics and information particular to that informant. Fourth, the teacher then shares the list of topics with the students to help focus their questions. Fifth, the teacher can prepare an interview that will be conducive to the needs of both the informant and the class. The second step is then the actual interview, which, with all the preparatory work, is more focused and productive.

Creating a Historical Context

When we partnered with a school to conduct an oral history project with the theme, "December 7, 1941," the teachers made it very clear in early discussions that the students would probably have a hard time asking questions around such a theme as they had little to no knowledge of that day. We arranged with the Arizona Memorial education department at Pearl Harbor to bring the classes to the museum to visit the memorial and museum and to have a private talk with several of the docents at the memorial who were survivors of that day.

The visit provided successful on several levels. Not only did the trip rouse the students' interest, but also the question-and-answer period with the survivors proved to be good training for the upcoming oral history interviews. Many parents took off from work that day to be chaperones in order to share this rare treat. The Arizona Memorial people were pleased with the visit, as they have been working at finding alternative ways to stimulate interest in the memorial and to contribute to the community.

JOURNAL RESPONSE QUESTIONS

A list of potential questions follows. This list was developed over time and with students in Hawai'i. Use as many or as few as apply and use them as jumping-off points to develop questions more suited to the students involved in the project.

Before Oral History Collection Begins

- What is an "oral history?"
- I think learning about history is important or unimportant because . . .
- I like/don't like talking with elderly people because . . .

After Oral History Collection

- I think learning about history is important or unimportant because . . .
- I like/don't like talking with elderly people because . . .
- Describe what is hard about this part of the process.
- When and why did you feel successful?
- When and why did you feel frustrated?
- What was the most important thing you learned that you never knew before?

OUTLINE OF THE PROCESS

Materials

    notebooks and pens/pencils

    tape recorders and/or video cameras

    interview guide cards

Suggested Time Frame

two interview sessions

What Are You Working Toward?

- a thoughtful and engaging dialogue between the oral history informant and the students
- students not reading questions, but listening to answers and creating new questions based on the answers
- oral history informants telling stories, relating memories and events, not reciting facts
- students making notes of stories of particular interest
- oral history informants relaxed and honest
- the students leading the questions, not the teacher

The Oral History Informant

> *The George L. story makes me think about the war and it makes me want to ask lots of questions.*
>
> —SIXTH GRADER, KANEʻOHE

Choosing an Oral History Informant

- A good informant:
    is comfortable talking with children;
    is patient and fills in details without always having to be asked;
    goes beyond simple "yes's" or "no's" for answers.
- Older relatives of students make good informants as they bring a familiarity and relaxed informality, which leads to a deeper interview.
- An older community member who has a deep connection with the history of the community can also be a good informant, as the students will come to see a new side to people they encounter every day, but know little about.
- Local museum docents, other faculty at the school, or retired police or fire personnel are also possibilities.
- Contacting a local retirement home or senior citizens' organization might provide some real gems.

Preparing Your Oral History Informant

- Let your informant know the project theme, the kinds of questions your students are developing, the way the interview will be conducted, where it will be conducted, and that you will be recording the interview.

- Conduct an initial introductory interview with the informant. In this introductory interview, seek basic information about the informant's life, telling the informant that this will aid the children in focusing their questions and the interview in general.

- Ask your informant to start the actual interview with a story of something that happened to them as a child. This creates a warm connection between your students and the informant.

- Ask your informant to bring photographs, treasured mementos, or other objects that might help the students understand and visualize the events being discussed.

- Encourage your informant to involve the students and to actively demonstrate work, play, or other activities. Any concrete activities will give the students a more tangible experience, as well as material they can use for their scenes and short plays.

- Give the informant the power to call on students to ask questions.

- Ask whether the informant is willing to share personal memories or stories. Such questions might include: sad memories, personal disappointments, values and principles, dating, courtship, marriage, and deaths in the family.

- Have the informant use a prearranged gesture or signal to cue you if students get too anxious or too fast with questions or they are uncomfortable with any questions.

- Be sure you get permission from your informant to use their stories and memories to create your scenes and short plays.

Preparing for the Interview Session

- Give a good amount of information to your students about your informant (name, birthplace, marriage status, number of children, and the like). If you give this very basic information before the interview, the students will not dwell on it.

- Share the overall topics particular to your interviewee with your students. Childhood incidents and memories, special achievements, interesting jobs held when young, any historical events he was a part of, and so on.

- The more tangible the reality, the deeper the students' investment in the situation. Pictures, stories, videos, music, and props are very useful at this stage. A trip to a museum or borrowing a museum education box with implements and clothing is a great enhancement to entering the world of the characters. Often the exploration engages young people enough to motivate research about the situation as they are exploring it. The research gives them more information about the characters and their ways of living, working, and playing. Books, encyclopedias, and videos can give students a good introduction and better prepare them for what they might be hearing and asking about.

- Create timelines of the period of your informant or the theme for the project. To understand and practice the idea of timelines, start with a class timeline, outlining the past week or month of your class. Illustrate it on the blackboard, or possibly butcher paper (in preparation for the students creating their own).

Monday	Tuesday	Wednesday	Thursday	Friday
Monthly math test	Learning Internet in computer class	Teacher's birthday	Field trip to see a play	Special assembly

- After creating the class timeline, students create personal timelines.
  - Using butcher paper or several sheets of regular paper taped together, students draw a line straight down the middle.
  - Students divide the line with a mark for each year of their lives. Encourage the students to spread the marks equally along the horizontal line.
  - Students label each mark with years, starting from the year they were born all the way to the present year. They can also add their age at each of the marks.
  - Students think about the special events of their lives: memorable trips or vacations, special parties, the first day at school, being in the hospital, discovering a great place to play with friends, learning to ride a bicycle or play a sport, a first homerun, or starring in a community or school play. Students write each of the events under the line in the year it happened.
  - Students partner up, compare, and share timelines.

- Students take their timelines home and ask their parents to help fill it in further.
- Students create a timeline for the class oral history informant.
  - Students fill in the years and the age of the informant and anything else the class knows about her.
  - When interviewing the informant, students fill in the timeline as they ask questions related to the timeline:

    What are the most significant events in your life?

    When did each occur?

    What is your earliest memory?
  - After the interview, students fill in the timeline as completely as possible.
- Stage mock interviews in the classroom before the formal interviews with the oral history informant. (See Chapter 3.)
- Remind students to be considerate. Some questions they ask may touch on painful or sensitive memories. If your informant wishes to avoid a subject, let him do so.
- Encourage students to note particularly interesting stories and golden moments they hear during the interview.
- Confirm the interview time and length and remind your informant to bring along pictures or objects that might help illustrate memories.

The First Interview Session

- Set up tables for small groups of students. Give each table of students a theme or topic to be responsible for. This ensures that informants are not subjected to the same questions repeatedly. Allow each table group to ask questions for a short amount of time.
- Plan on the interview taking forty-five to sixty minutes.
- Set up some kind of recording device. This allows the students the chance to freely pose questions and follow-up questions without having to worry about writing down the information. Establish rules for asking questions and listening to answers. Students often get too excited by the process and want to ask all the questions right away without listening to the answers.
- Make sure to test the equipment before the interview so you are certain it works properly. Moreover, make sure that you have fresh batteries or that you can plug the equipment into an outlet.

- Try to anticipate when you are coming to the end of a tape. If a tape ends in the middle of an answer, change the tape immediately, and then repeat the question so that the answer can be rerecorded in its entirety.
- Share the following with your students:
  - Start with easy questions.
  - Don't interrupt or attempt to correct the person you are interviewing.
  - Do not worry if the informant stops speaking and there is silence. Sometimes the person is thinking about what to say next. Wait patiently, and you will find they will begin speaking soon. Do not be too quick with another question. Allow the person time to think. Try not to interrupt.
  - Remember that thinking back on the past will sometimes bring sad or uncomfortable memories. Be sensitive and kind. If the person looks uncomfortable, ask if she would like to continue talking on the topic or go on to another question.

After the Interview

- Send thank-you notes to your informant (and maybe pictures of the class with the informant).
- With your informant's permission, place copies of your interview in the school library.
- Be sure to invite the informants to the final performance!

Follow-up Discussion with Students

After the initial interview . . .

- Review the tape.
- Discuss the good and bad questions.
- Discuss the golden moments and interesting discoveries.

But now I know why we truly have to do this. I really think this town is very important to the people that live here.
—SIXTH GRADER, WAHIAWA

Choosing Stories from the Oral History Interviews

- When selecting which stories to develop into scenes and short plays, make sure they contain some form of dramatic conflict—a situation where two or more characters strive for opposing goals. Without conflict, there is no drama. The presentation will lack any sense of forward motion and will not be interesting. A story that suggests some type of closure or resolution can give your presentation a strong shape. If a story has a strong dramatic core and a solid ending, it is easy to shape the rest of the presentation, even the beginning.

- If students are given strong characters with clear wants and needs and significant action or actions to achieve these objectives, the students will have more than enough to create their own dialogue and action during the devising sequence step.

Examples of Oral History Topics from the HTY Project

- Kapuna "P"—A ghost dog that frightens people on the Pali Highway; a disappearing lady who "magically" appears and disappears on roadways or in the backseat of cars
- Mrs. "P"—A conflict regarding the development of houses on sacred land
- Mr. "J. R."—The reluctance of visiting students to enter a taro patch for a classroom assignment
- Mr. "I"—Working as a teenager in the mountains planting trees and creating trails; hiking down the mountain each day to play baseball
- Mr. "R"—Growing up and working in the plantations; spooky stories told on the plantations; the real tragedies and the daily work schedule

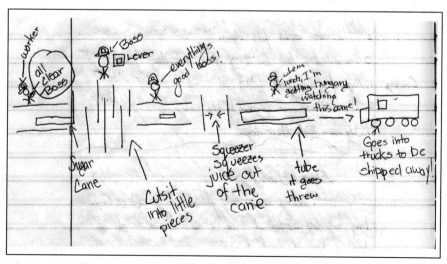

Figure 4–1.
A student's drawing based on information gathered from an oral history interview

Examples of Oral History Stories from the HTY Project

- "When Pearl Harbor was bombed our family built a bomb shelter while the children packed food and water. We hid in the bomb shelter and waited for 3 days. After that we got to go back inside our house."

- "When he went to school he said he remembered that in the bathroom the boys always listened to the girls through the wall. One time there were so many boys listening through the wall that the wall came down!"

- "There was a big flood in Kaneʻohe. The stream back there filled up high with water. Logs got jammed up and so the water went high over the edge. They were visiting friends over the Pali and when they came back late at night, they could not get back home. The water came up on their car and they had to crawl onto the roof of the car to wait for help."

- "I was driving to work when I accidentally ran over a mongoose. When I got to work, I saw my friends. I went to hang my lunch on the tree. I saw someone's lunch on the ground. When I started working, I saw some people taking beans from other people's bags. I saw this girl, and she was so slow. Then we went into some hills. The same girl was rolling down the hills. We were all laughing. But luckily she wasn't hurt. Then we went to eat our lunches. The girl was eating the lunch that was on the ground. I guess the mongoose ate it."

- "They sent him to be a water boy on the plantation when he was eight. He got the water by the stream that was clean, clear, and cold. He loved being a water boy because then he didn't have to work in the fields. He used to dry corn and melt cheese to trap birds and raise them."

- "When [Mrs. O and her family] were running to hide in the cave [in the Philippines], some people were shot from the airplanes. Then they had to live there, but the water was outside the cave and people were scared to get it. They had to watch for the airplanes. Some of her friends died because of the war."

- "I lied to get into the army. I didn't like school and all I did at home was help my mother with the laundry business. So, when I was fifteen, I told them I was seventeen. They gave me papers to sign up, because if you were under eighteen, you have to have your parent's permission. I told my mother the men said it was okay that I was only fifteen if she signed the papers. She didn't mind. She was from Korea. She only spoke Korean, so when the men asked her if it was okay, I translated. Many years later I told the truth, but my superior officers said it was alright and I stayed in the army for many years."

- "He told us they had to carry a gas mask all of the time. And some days they had to test it. Everyone, even kids, had to go to the school. One room was full with gas. They put on their masks, walked through the room. Before they left, the people made them take off the mask. It was to be sure that kids always remembered to carry their masks. All the people came out of the room with tears."

Researching the Context

Students often imagine the informant in a world much like their own, so when they create scenes and short plays from the material, they will incorporate television, videos, video games, and the like. Besides the pictures and artifacts the informants bring in to accompany the interview, other research might be conducted to help students gain a deeper understanding of the time period, the community, and the overall material of daily life of the oral histories. Reading accounts of the time period, seeing pictures of the community, and the fashions and material of life at that time will greatly help students in their imaginative shaping of the scenes and short plays. Following are places to go to find out more about the time period, the specific community, and to gain an overall understanding of the daily life of the informants.

- Internet
- library
- museum
- historical and conservation societies
- historical sites, federal parks
- university collections—newspapers, magazines, radio recordings
- government records
- grandparents—the old boxes stored in the attic, basement, or garage

Oral History Resources

My History Is America's History guidebook by the National Endowment for the Humanities. You can obtain a copy by calling 1-877-NEH-HISTORY or at www.myhistory.org.

Oral History in the Secondary School Classroom by Barry A. Lanman and George L. Mehaffy.

How to Do Oral History by the Center for Oral History, University of Hawai'i at Manoa. 1-808-956-6259.

Also, see the Bibliography.

5

Devising Sequence

It also made me think that I was very smart and creative because I was making a play and it makes me feel great when I think back knowing that I helped create this play and that I put in little parts of this play. I feel awesome because all of this was a play that us children created without following a paper or a script.

—SIXTH GRADER, KANE'OHE

AT A GLANCE

Students apply the techniques they learned in the drama skill-building step, exploring and creating scenes and short plays from the collected oral histories.

GOALS/OBJECTIVES

- to have students explore collected oral histories
- to have students come to know a piece of history more intimately
- to devise scenes and short plays from the collected oral histories
- to help students appreciate the power of stories to instill pride in one's self and heritage
- to enhance students' oral communication skills
- to enhance students' understanding of how to shape and develop a storyline

INSIGHT

Oral histories are personal memories. To try to re-create them exactly would be difficult at best. To use them as a jumping-off point for exploration of human behavior makes the process much more challenging and engaging for young people. The process of creating an original scene or short play based on an oral history gives students the chance for an intimate and in-depth study of communication, human behavior, and their own understanding of human relationships. As young people come to understand their place in the world through both formal (at home, in the classroom) and informal (on the playground) role-play, the creating and acting out of the oral histories offers the teacher a starting point for discussions related not only to human behavior but also conflict resolution, behavior management, race, and gender relations.

All this is accomplished through experimentation. Offering young people the chance to brainstorm, experiment, explore, and devise original scenes and short plays really gets them to think about all these issues and challenges all their creative muscles. They end up creating some wonderful scenes and short plays.

JOURNAL RESPONSE QUESTIONS

A list of potential questions follows. This list was developed over time and with students in Hawai'i. Use as many or as few as apply and use them as jumping-off points to develop questions more suited to the students involved in the project.

- How did the situation you acted out make you feel and why?
- What did the drama make you think about?
- What part of your scene do you hope to improve on?
- How did the drama classes help you this week?
- What did you do in drama class this week that made you proud of yourself?
- What was the most important thing you learned this week that you never knew before?
- When and why did you feel successful today/this week?
- When and why did you feel frustrated today/this week?
- How did your participation contribute to today's/this week's class(es)? What changes would you like to make for yourself tomorrow/next week?
- In what activities did you participate as a leader this week? What did you do that made you a leader? How did the other students in your group respond to you as a leader?
- Who in your class made some important contributions in class this week? What did he do that you felt was important?

- How well did your group work together this week? What did the group do that you think was good?
- How do you solve problems if your group does not agree? Give an example.
- Did you ever compromise and give up what you wanted to do? How did that turn out?
- How can your group work better as team? What can you do to help the group?
- How do you think drama class went this week? What did the class do that was successful? What did the class do that was not so successful? What could your class improve on?

I think it could be better if I said to Unoluto "I'm not going to be here for family dinner because me and my friend Shantey the nurse have a meeting at the hospital I think I have to sub for Dr. (anyone) he called in sick."

—FIFTH GRADER, KANEʻOHE

OUTLINE OF THE PROCESS

Materials

copies of the chosen oral histories; chart paper; markers

props as needed for the developing storylines; musical instruments as needed

Support Materials

period information that offers a historical context for the oral histories—books, pictures, objects, videos

Suggested Time Frame

The sessions should be flexible in length and duration. The suggested sequence of activities breaks the process into small steps so that all the groups within a particular class can work simultaneously. If each story has an equal number of scenes, this can help control the devising process. It is important to note, however, that students and groups move at different speeds. Some may need more time to discuss, experiment, get past embarrassment, reflect, and redo.

What Are You Working Toward?

The atmosphere of fun built up during the drama portion of the process should continue during the devising even on the days it is extremely important to finish a scene or polish the movement sequence. If the students do not enjoy this process, they will get very little out of it and eventually have nothing to share or of which to feel proud. Continue to make time to play, returning to favorite activities and warm-ups before beginning the work of each session.

Second, as in the drama portion, the students should be "engaged in the moment" both of generating ideas and shaping them. As they are searching, they may be tentative about fully investing themselves in the drama task. An all too common response is the instructor giving the students the "answer" (lines of dialogue to say or overly specific actions to do), assuming the tentativeness indicates the students do not know what they are doing. However, if they are given the opportunity to gain a full understanding of the story or situation they are exploring, they will be able to fully develop dialogue, action, and, eventually, a scene.

There is truly a difference between a child performing something an adult has prescribed and one engaged in the creation of the moment. When a child is "engaged in the moment" the work is electrifying. The audience is no longer looking at how cute the child is, but are amazed by how intent the young person is on the reality of the scene or short play.

Occurrences to look out for that indicate a student is not truly engaged include:

- Unreal sounding or "stiff" dialogue. This means too much of the material has been prescribed or they have merely been asked to learn words and have not been given the chance to understand the context of those words. Young people memorize quickly, but that does not mean they understand quickly. They are merely trying to remember what they are saying without truly understanding why they are saying it. They can say it, but they do not always know why they are saying it. Having placed all their energies on memorizing words, they get fixated on the tiny mistakes ("Jenny didn't say that right"), which throws off the whole scene. It is not the words that are important, but the meaning. Even if the lines of dialogue are scripted, the emphasis should always be on meaning and not on the "right" words.

- Lack of attention on the action. This means that students have merely learned what they are supposed to do and are waiting around for their turn. When asked what they are doing, students commonly respond, "Waiting to say my line." Once again, they are not invested in the reality of the moment. Whether they are improvising the dialogue and action (which immediately negates the "waiting for my line" problem) or have memorized a script, the situation needs to be more deeply explored and understood.

Occurrences to watch for indicating the students are engaged include:

- students closely examining the oral histories, teasing out the interesting and dramatic details;
- students creating dramatic images, scenes, or small plays full of characters, action, problems, and detailed events;
- students focusing on the basic properties of a good story to help dramatize their chosen oral histories.

Steps in the Process

Use the Steps in the Process guidelines outlined in the Chapter 2.

Considering Structures for Devising

There are a variety of ways in which the oral history material can be presented, including simple still images, still images accompanied by narration, a series of still images with or without narration, pantomimed scenes with or without narration, single scenes framed by narrative, and complete short plays (consisting of any number of scenes). Which is the best choice is dependent on several factors: the oral history material, the amount of time allotted to the development of the scenes or short plays, and the ability level of the students involved in the process.

When discussing with the students how to best structure the oral histories into dramatic presentations, more than likely students will want to create plays full of dialogue and action. This is because most students have had little opportunity to explore, use, or see the other types of structures. Although the teacher should not decide for the students which structure is best, the teacher should be an active contributor in the conversation, guiding students to think through which choice or choices might best work for them or their chosen oral history material.

The teacher should also be an active observer, noting whether students or groups of students are having difficulty creating their images, scenes, or short plays. The teacher can offer students alternative structures or techniques that might better suit them or their stories.

Most students should have little problem creating still images or even pantomimed scenes. It is when simple stories need to be fleshed out into scenes and short plays, creating dialogue and action that supports characters and plotlines, that the process can become challenging for some students or groups.

For this reason, the process for devising as detailed in this chapter involves several steps. Instead of jumping directly into creating or writing dialogue and trying to imagine and shape entire scenes or storylines, this process encourages starting with still images (or tableaux) and slowly adding simple action, narrative, and finally character action and dialogue. In this way, the process can be stopped at any step that seems doable and comfortable for the students. The steps can also be repeated, expanded upon, and/or creatively altered to best suit the students, timeframe, and oral histories.

Overall Devising Approach

Thank you for letting us make up our own play. This is really cool to be in a play that you make up. Everybody gets to be in it. It is also fun to imagine to do something. Like riding in a bus. I could almost feel the bus shaking and crashing. I like those feelings. That's what makes acting fun.

—FIFTH GRADER, KANE'OHE

First, students should decide upon the storyline of their scene or short play. As stated previously, the storyline should feature a conflict at its core. The storyline is shaped around the conflict, from setup of the situation to the resolution of the conflict.

The conflict is built around the intentions or goals of the characters within the story. What the characters pursue and how they pursue it should put each of them in direct conflict with their own limitations or another character of the story. When students can identify what their character is pursuing, they will be able to build the dialogue and action of their scene as the dialogue and action communicate the character's intention or goal. The various characters' goals put them in opposition to each other, which fuels the development of dialogue and action.

As students work on the scenes, they will get lost in the minutiae of the facts and situations of the oral histories. Throughout the devising sequence, it is important to keep them on track. The instructor should ask questions regarding the characters' intentions and goals:

- What is it each character wants, needs, or is pursuing?
- Who does the character need to help him?
- How does the character get her to help?
- What does each character need to do (action) to achieve the intention or goal?
- What are the obstacles the character is facing?
- What are the various ways the character might overcome the obstacle?

The instructor should ask questions about the central conflict:

- What is the conflict?
- Why does it exist?
- How does the conflict keep the characters from achieving their intentions and goals?
- How do the characters feel about the conflict?
- How can the conflict get worse before it gets better?
- What choices can the characters make to solve or overcome the conflict?

The devising should also be about setting up the environment of the story. How can the students use their bodies and voices to create the various atmospheres and environments? If a scene takes place on a street, a group of students can be other people on the street, another group can provide vocal sound effects of a street, and others might be fire hydrants and lampposts. Even without a realistic set, the scene can be very impressive, very engaging for the students, and very quick and simple to transform into any other atmosphere or environment.

Basic Steps for Devising Scenes and Short Plays

- Groups discover the heart of their chosen story by creating a single tableau.
- Groups discover their chosen story's sequence by creating a series of tableaux highlighting important events.
- Groups demonstrate their understanding of the story sequence by narrating the tableaux series.
- Groups explore the characters' intentions and relationships through improvisation.
- Groups discover more avenues for exploration by sharing and evaluating their developing scenes or short plays.
- Groups create narration and titles to frame their short plays.

Ongoing Devising Reflection

Each time a group shares a developing scene or scenes, the whole class should reflect on the choices made and how the group sharing might develop their ideas further. Questions that might be asked follow. Please note this is a list developed over time and use with students in Hawai'i. Use as many or as few as apply, and use them as jumping-off points to develop questions more suited to the scenes being created.

Instructor Asks Questions of the Sharing Group

- How do you feel it went?
- Did you stay in it?
- Did you make it important to you?
- Did you make strong choices and build the story together?
- What moments were strong? What lines? Actions?
- What could you have done differently to make the character's need stronger?

Instructor Asks Questions of the Audience

- Did the participants listen to each other as well as talk?
- Where did the participants clearly work together as a whole?
- What moments were strong? What lines? Actions?
- What could they have done differently?

Students Evaluate Themselves and Their Participation in Their Story

- I thought I did a good job on/with . . .
- I think it would be better if I . . .

Students Evaluate Their Contribution to Their Story

- Today (or in this practice run) I added/tried . . .
- I think I could do more with . . .

Students Evaluate the Other Members of Their Group

- I think (name) did a good job, because . . .

Students Offer Constructive Criticism to Each Other

- I think (group name) did especially well with . . .
- I think (group name) need to concentrate on . . .

Students Suggest Ideas for Continued Exploration

- I think (group name) could do more with . . .

As the scenes become richer and more detailed, turning into short plays, the questions asked should become more focused and specific.

The Story

- Was the story clearly communicated? What was missing or extra?
- What more might the group do to make the story clearer?

The Characters

- Did the group members stay in their character throughout the sharing?

- Were the characters clear and focused on an intention?
- How might the performers clarify what their character is trying to achieve?

The Dialogue

- Did the words the performers used help communicate their intention and the story?
- Did the dialogue stay focused on the story? What might have been said that seemed unnecessary?
- Did the dialogue seem too modern?
- What else might the different characters need to say to help clarify their intention or the overall story?

The Action

- Did the physical actions seem realistic or in keeping with the story?
- Was there a nice balance of action and dialogue? Which should the group explore more?
- What might the performers add or remove?

The Rhythm

- Were the scenes rushed, slow, or had a good rhythm?
- Did the rhythm of the scene or short play match the mood?
- How might the rhythm be changed to capture the different moods of the story?

Preparations for Devising

A wide variety of events, adventures, stories, and anecdotes generally come up in the interviews. The job of choosing which to use can be challenging, as much more material is collected than can ever really be made into a dramatic presentation.

Choosing Stories

Choose stories from the collected oral histories as a class. Look for stories that . . .

- are dramatically viable: they have a central conflict;
- are action based: they are not just people sitting around talking;
- have a clear central character or characters that journey through the conflict;
- suggest a clear resolution to the conflict or clear closure;
- can easily be broken down into scenes.

Examples

Mrs. G

Mrs. G shared brief experiences of growing up. Three particular experiences caught the students' imaginations. All three centered around life after the attack on December 7, 1941.

Mrs. G told of the evening's curfew and blackouts that the whole community had to obey. In her case, she was responsible for taking care of her little brothers and sisters who were all confined to a single, dark room at night. Mrs. G explained how she made up games with her younger siblings to keep their minds off reality. Second, she told of wanting to join the army, but when she asked her father, "He gave me an emphatic *no!*" she explained. Third, she mentioned that, because she was eighteen years old at the time of the war, she was conscripted to work on compiling gun belts for the war effort.

Mr. L and Dr. H

One class interviewed two different informants. Mr. L told some wonderful stories of growing up. One story explained how Mr. L was trouble in school, causing a variety of different kinds of problems for the teacher. Eventually he dropped out of school or, as he humorously described it, "escaped."

With Dr. H, the students liked stories of his childhood adventures swimming in the local lake (as it is polluted today), playing along the railroad tracks (there are no more trains), and eating pineapples right in the pineapple fields (considered stealing today).

Planning the Dramatization

Discuss the chosen stories as a class.

- Write a title for each story on separate pieces of chart paper.
- On the chart paper . . .
  - list characters found in each story;
  - list all the places or settings within each story;
  - note the main character's intention or goal;
  - note the conflict to the main character's intention;
  - note the resolution to the conflict.

Examples

Mrs. G

Curfew/Blackouts

> *Characters:* Mrs. G, her family
> *Setting:* home
> *Intention:* to help her younger siblings
> *Conflict:* (in this one the class suggested maybe the siblings wanted to go outside to play)
> *Resolution:* Mrs. G makes up games for her siblings

Joining the Army

> *Characters:* Mrs. G, her father
> *Setting:* home
> *Intention:* to join the army
> *Conflict:* her father says no
> *Resolution:* she didn't join the army

Making Gun Belts

> *Characters:* Mrs. G, other workers
> *Setting:* base
> *Intention:* (the class decided this wasn't very clear)
> *Conflict:* (the class discovered there wasn't any)
> *Resolution:* (the class discovered there wasn't any)

Mr. L and Dr. H

Playing with Friends

> *Characters:* Dr. H and friends
> *Setting:* Outside at the lake, on the railroad tracks, and in the pineapple field
> *Intention:* ("to have a good time," the class suggested)
> *Conflict:* (the class decided there wasn't any)
> *Resolution:* (the class decided there wasn't any)

At School

> *Characters:* Mr. L, his friends, the teacher, other classmates
> *Setting:* school
> *Intention:* to avoid schoolwork
> *Conflict:* causing trouble with the teacher
> *Resolution:* Mr. L quit school

Review the breakdown of scenes. If possible, break each story into an equal number of scenes.

- Breaking each story down into an equal number of scenes may force you to skip some "funny" or "interesting" scenes, but making all the chosen stories equal in length will help in the devising process. All the student groups will be able to work simultaneously and, ideally, finish at the same time.

- Focusing on a simple number of scenes also focuses the work of the students on the central conflict of the scene or short play they are developing. The simplest breakdown might look like this:

  Scene One introduces the situation and the characters.

  Scene Two sets up the conflict.

  Scene Three develops the situation and conflict.

  Scene Four resolves the conflict.

- If necessary, add narration only to set a context (place, character, and basic situation) for the scene (see Adding Narration and Titles p. 103).

Examples

Discussing Mrs. G's Stories with the Students

The students, of course, wanted to use the blackout, joining the army, and the gun belt experiences, so we discussed how none of them actually presented a full story. The students decided that the joining the army experience at least had some conflict to it, so we started with that story. As we talked about how to set up the situation, to understand that Mrs. G wanted to join the army, one young girl suggested we set Scene One at the gun belt–making place and have her be with her friends or other workers. The suggestion for the end of the story was to have Mrs. G either discover her place was taking care of her younger siblings or have her father explain how she was needed at home.

The Resulting Outline of a Mrs. G Story

Scene One: Gail works with friends/colleagues on making gun belts. Gail and friends discuss how they might be most useful in the war. Gail discovers and/or decides she is interested in joining the army.

Scene Two: Gail is at home, working with her father in the yard. She brings up her interest in joining the army. Her father ends the conversation saying, "I'll think about it."

continued from previous page

Scene Three: Gail discovers, while working on the gun belts again, that some of her friends or colleagues are joining up.

Scene Four: During the evening's blackout, after Gail has taken care of her younger siblings, she asks her father again. He says no, Gail is needed to take care of the family.

Discussing Mr. L's and Dr. H's Stories with the Students

The students wanted to use the material from both of these gentlemen. As the list of games Dr. H and his friends played does not amount to much dramatically, the question the students faced was how to best utilize the material so it had a purpose. In the discussion, a few students suggested the childhood activities and games be used as a precursor to the school story of Mr. L, setting up general life in the community. Having a variety of short scenes could help establish a sense of what young people did together in that time period and place, and prepare the audience for the story of a young man and his friends.

The Resulting Outline of Mr. L and Dr. H Stories

Scene One: Several different groups of students create tableaux and brief action scenes (accompanied by music) that show the variety of games and activities in which young people of the time participated.

Scene Two: Transitioning right out of the first scene, one young man (Mr. L) and his friends reluctantly decide to head off to school.

Scene Three: At school, the young man causes trouble for the teacher, getting some of his friends in trouble as well. The young man and his friends are sent to the principal.

Scene Four: The young man encourages his friends to sneak out of school. At the end, only he does.

Creating Devising Ensembles

Depending on how well the class works together in small groups, there are a couple of ways to create working ensembles to begin the devising work.

Small Ensembles

Students choose which story they prefer. At this stage, ignore whether there are enough characters or too many in the story of choice. The process of devising will adjust that. It is better if the students work on a story they like than be assigned one because a group needs more people.

Whole-Class Ensemble

The class picks a story that will accommodate the whole class. In this way of working, students occasionally break into small groups within the bigger story with more focused assignments around particular actions or activities instead of a multiple scene short play.

Example

A class picked a story of village life in the Philippines during World War II. The village was created by small groups of students, each creating the action of particular jobs within the community. One group worked with the animals, another planted and harvested taro, another tended the vegetable patch, and the last cleaned house. These activities were explored in two ways. First, individuals within the small groups decided which particular activity he would do. Second, the group worked out the coordination of their actions (one dug, another planted, a third watered). After sharing, the groups then began to create dialogue. A discussion then followed, exploring the types of problems they might encounter within their group, and dialogue and particular character traits were developed. The whole group was then pieced together. On a predetermined cue, one group at a time completed their partial scene.

Devising—First Steps

In the first steps of this process, it is expected students' focus will wander. Remind them to stay in character as they explore and share their developing scenes and short plays. The reminders should happen either before students begin or after they end. Do not stop the exploration. Students need the time to explore fully in order to take control of their developing scene or short play. Reflecting on an exploration afterward helps students understand the process of developing and shaping an idea. If students are stopped during a practice session, they begin to shy away from taking chances, afraid they will be stopped and corrected. As has been noted, devising is not about right and wrong, it is about discovering and understanding. Students need to discover what works best for them before they come to understand how to best present their discoveries. Once students have become comfortable in their understanding and control of a scene or story, only then is it time to concern them with how the audience understands the story.

The first few times the scenes and short plays are shared, they will most likely be far from perfect. This should be expected and planned for. It takes time to explore, discover, understand, reexplore, rediscover, deepen the understanding, and put all that knowledge into practice. Each step in this process should be seen as just that: a step. After a practice or sharing, the drama instructor should note the successes and then offer suggestions and questions that will help guide the students to further discoveries. If too much time is spent pointing out what did not work, students will become frustrated and unenthused about developing their ideas any further. It is not advisable to prescribe specific lines of dialogue or action at this point either. That sets up a situation where students are dependent on someone else for their ideas, which completely defeats the point of devising.

Developing a Short Play Structure

Groups create tableaux.

- Groups create one tableau at a time for each scene in the story.
- All groups simultaneously practice the tableaux. On the instructor's cue, all groups have five seconds to make their tableaux.
- With each new tableau, practice all previous tableaux. Allow about five seconds to change from one tableau to another.
- Groups share their sequence of tableaux with the class.
- Students discuss the effectiveness of each tableau or sequence.
- Groups redo their tableaux as necessary.
- Groups share tableaux again.

Exploring the Short Play Sequence

Groups storytell (narrate) the tableaux.

- Groups decide whether one student will storytell the whole sequence of tableaux or several students will share the storytelling duties.
- Groups work on one tableau/scene at a time.
- All groups simultaneously practice tableau. On the instructor's cue, all groups have five seconds to make their tableaux, then all storytellers talk simultaneously.
- With each new tableau, practice all previous tableaux. Allow five seconds to change from one tableau to another, after the storytellers have finished.
- Groups share their sequence of tableaux and storytelling with the rest of the class.
- Students discuss the effectiveness of the tableaux and storytelling.
- Groups redo their work as necessary.
- Groups share tableaux again.

Creating Dialogue and Action

Today was fun because all the cows drowned because of the flood! I was one of the cows too! The neighbors had to save the cows from the water and some of the cows did not get saved!

We practiced the stream scene too. When the waterfall stopped and there was a log in the way then the log fell down and all the water came down so we ran away. Then Dane came out because he was hiding from the rain. Chris had to take Jordan's place because Jordan was doing his Hawai'ian music.

—Fifth grader, Kane'ohe

Creating a "Script"

When first creating the material, do not write down any of the dialogue. Writing down the dialogue too early will "freeze" the story and turn many of the students into "stiff" performers, actors who are merely trying to remember the dialogue. Instead of writing down the dialogue, students improvise and develop new ideas, which will mean more dialogue each time they practice. With continued exploration, the students will gain both confidence and a good understanding of their characters and the situations. That confidence will encourage the students to continue. This, in turn, will produce better and more natural dialogue. This is central to the project: confidence in self and understanding of the subject matter.

Initial Challenges

Scenes may be very short to begin with. This simply means the students have not fully explored the possibilities yet; they are still thinking of what they must say to get to the next part of the story. Students often "run out of ideas" or stick to one-word lines of dialogue. After each practice or devising session, ask the members of the group about the characters, the characters' intentions or goals, the problem the characters are facing. Asking questions is the same as challenging the students to contribute more ideas.

Students may talk all at the same time during the devising. Let them. In the early stages of devising, it does not matter if they can be understood easily or if the whole scene or short play makes sense. Individual students need the time to process their place within the scene. If students are allowed to talk only one at a time in the early stages, the most talkative students will dominate. The shyest/quietest students can become strong contributors if they feel safe as they explore and contribute ideas in the early stages of the devising.

A Note on Jokes

In this day of television laugh tracks, many people think a scene or play is not very good if it does not have laughs. Often, when working improvisationally, participants throw in funny lines of dialogue to get a reaction from the audience. For actors trying hard to create something worthwhile on the spot, the temptation to throw in a joke or a funny line of dialogue can be great.

Discuss this with the students. Merely making an audience laugh does not necessarily serve the drama. The question to be explored is, "How does the joke or funny line help the audience understand the character or the situation better?"

> *Today I put in another line, "Mommy I'm scared I don't like the roof, it's tall and dark and there is rushing water all over the place." My teacher liked that line.*
>
> —FIFTH GRADER, KANEʻOHE

Developing Scenes

Groups flesh out scenes using dialogue and action.

- As students develop dialogue for their scenes, encourage trying all ideas. All are valid in the devising sessions.
- Groups develop action for the scenes in the same way as the dialogue. Do not let them set it too early. Let them experiment and explore.

> *Today in HTY [Honolulu Theatre for Youth], we learned to put more action words in our scenes. The scene that I'm in (the flooded family) it isn't that long, it's actually pretty short, but we have some good lines that we make up as we go.*
>
> —FIFTH GRADER, KANEʻOHE

- Groups work on one scene at a time.
- All groups simultaneously practice the scenes.
- With each new scene, practice all previous scenes.
- Groups share the developing scenes.
  - Have each group share each scene with the rest of the class as they develop them.
  - Videotape the sharings so groups can evaluate their own developing scenes.
  - Students discuss the effectiveness of the developing scenes.
  - Groups redo their work as necessary.
  - Share the scenes again.

Note: If students have a hard time thinking up dialogue, have other students in the class volunteer to step in and try it. Having two or three others try the scene will give the original student more ideas to work with and create a supportive and creative environment.

Focusing the Dialogue and Action

You have to know about your character. You have to know what your character wants, and why, and you have to be loud, try not to laugh, and pay attention.

—SIXTH GRADER, WAHIAWA

After a period of exploring and experimenting with dialogue and action, groups set their dialogue and action.

- Groups choose the strongest dialogue with which they have been experimenting.
- Groups decide upon key dialogue that needs to be said to convey the important information of the scene or story.
- Groups discuss the order of the dialogue.

This is my new line from today "HaHaHa look that Hawai'ian girl rolling down the hill. HaHaHa. And remember yesterday she was picking the Kona Coffee so slow. And I forget to tell her to put her lunch at the top of the tree."

—SIXTH GRADER, KALIHI

Focusing Activities

One-Word Dialogue
If students are talking too much, have them play out the scene with each student allowed to say only one word each time they have a line. This can teach the economy of expression.

First Line, Last Line
If groups seem unsure when scenes start or stop, set the first and last line of the scene. The first line breaks the opening tableau of a scene and the last line signals the closing tableau.

Title
Assigning each scene a title can focus the students on the central issue of the scene.

Framing the Scenes and Short Plays

After the scenes have become more concrete, groups create opening and closing tableaux for each scene. Having tableaux that frame each individual scene helps in many ways.

- It gives the instructor greater control during practice. The instructor can tell if a group is ready to start a scene when all the members of that group are in the tableau.
- It gives students an anchor. They will be able to know when it is time to start and when they must work toward an agreed upon end.
- It makes it easier to get to the heart of the scene. By starting with a tableau, the characters in the scenes do not all need to enter and exit. The characters can already be in the midst of the action of a scene, therefore making each scene start more dynamically.
- It is easy for the narrator to know when a scene has stopped.
- It lets the audience focus on one thing at a time, either the scene or the narrator.
- It gives strong cues to the audience that a story has started or ended.
- It allows students to easily transition in and out of character.

Adding Narration and Titles

Narration

Narration should only be used to help set up a story or situation. Telling too much of the story in narration undercuts the conflict of the scene or short play. When presenting narration students should be in the role of a character, presenting the narration from that character's point of view. Characters can be from within or outside the stories. Their narration can frame an individual series of scenes or short plays or link all short plays within a class. The narration is also a way to connect the short plays to the project theme. Examples of successful narrator characters include: radio broadcasters, students writing homework at home (the oral history project), students presenting a history report to the class, the oral history informants telling their stories, and the characters within the stories telling their story through diaries or journals.

Examples

Radio

- "This is Kellie from Headline Radio saying come back with us to the past, to days of yesteryear, as we share and experience significant events in the lives of Hawai'i's people. Shyla-Lyn has the first story."
- "This is Shyla-lyn reporting live from Headline News. What would you do if there was a fire in your house? Well, here's a story that will tell you what to do when there's a fire!"
- "Just in! This is Moira reporting live at Kamehameha Boarding school. Did you ever wonder what kids did at boarding school? Well, at Kamehameha plenty of kids are doing chores and getting into a lot of mischief."
- "This is Deanne, live at Kane'ohe's neighborhood fruit stand, where usually it's 'Fruits, fruits for sale! Come here and get your fruits!' But today some people see smoke rising up from Pearl Harbor."

Character

- "Dear Diary, Today was my first day on the Kona Coffee picking. It was the most terrible day. These Filipino ladies were going so fast. I couldn't because if I picked too much green I'd be fired. We're only supposed to pick red. By the end of the day, my bag wasn't even halfway full, the other ladies got a 100 dollars because they filled the whole bag. I'll do better tomorrow, hopefully!"
- "Dear Diary, Today has been kind of good, but there were some fast workers. I was slowly picking the coffee beans one by one. Then I saw a person stealing coffee beans from someone's basket. When I went to get my lunch, I saw a mongoose run away with something. Meanwhile, I saw someone rolling down the hill. Everyone laughed at that person and then everyone went home."
- "Dear Diary, It was early in the morning. It was time to cut the cane. A person was cutting when a scorpion came by and stung the person. The person was very ill and he was yelling for help. When help came, he was running and tripping."
- "Dear Diary, Yesterday was amazing. A cowboy branded himself instead of the cow!"

Titles

Students give their scenes and short plays titles. Titles separate one short play from the next within an individual classroom. The titles can also be incorporated into the narration as a clean way to begin each new scene or short play.

Examples

Stealing the Family Car
> At Home
> At School
> Late at Night at Home
> The Flooded Car

Girls and Boys at the Stream
> At School
> At the Girls' Homes
> The Cow Pasture
> At the Stream

Trouble Awaits: The Boarding School
> Washing Clothes
> Prank
> Study Hall
> Toilets

Coffee Picker's Nightmare
> Hairy Spiders in the Hair
> Rolling Down the Hill
> The Mystery of My Missing Lunch
> Pay Day for Coffee Pickers

The Bombing of Pearl Harbor
> Shelter Hideout
>> Preparing
>> Hiding Out
> A Sad Good-bye
>> Dad Is Recruited
>> A Family Cries

Introductory Images and Sounds

As the theme of the project plays such an important role in the choice of the oral history informants, the interviews, and the dramatic presentations, introducing the theme in some creative way at the beginning of any performance can bring every scene, every group, and every class together in one grand thematic performance.

Original Song/Rap

Using the words and images originally explored in the theme brainstorming, individuals, small groups, or even the whole class might participate in putting together an original song or rap introducing the theme of the evening. Songs or raps can also be used as the narrative links.

Musical Montage

Creating a found objects orchestra (see Chapter 6) offers the chance for all class members to contribute musically in very simple ways. Using very simple rhythms and steady beats, whole sections of woodblocks, army boots, plastic buckets, and metal pipes can create an impressive musical montage that sets a mood or feeling for the evening.

Verbal/Image-Based Montage

A fun, quick, and eye-grabbing introduction can be cobbled together using key moments from the devised scenes and short plays. Each group of students picks one moment they believe best represents and creates a momentary mystery in their scene or presentation. Each group then quickly comes to the front of the performance area and holds a tableau for a few seconds as a line of dialogue, a title, or an overarching question is spoken. Then the next group does the same and so on until all the groups have presented their brief moment. Music can effectively underscore the montage.

6

Music and Movement

In the beginning of our play, we have a musical introduction with pipes, blocks, trashcan covers, sticks and taiko. It sounds really great. For movement we have steps where people wake up and then point at planes then turn into little planes then a big plane finally they split into two bombs and they blow up.

—SIXTH GRADER, WAHIAWA

AT A GLANCE

Students learn to play a variety of instruments, using the music to create mood for the scenes and transitions between stories. Students develop a basic movement vocabulary and devise ways to add movement to their scenes.

GOALS/OBJECTIVES

- to have students learn culturally specific musical instruments
- to have students develop a basic movement vocabulary
- to offer students the chance to explore parts of stories impossible in dialogue alone
- to augment the scenes and short plays using music and movement
- to have students develop nonverbal communication skills
- to create transitions between scenes and short plays using movement and/or music
- to help students appreciate the power of music and movement to communicate meaning
- to have students explore a full range of art forms

INSIGHT

The Japanese artist Zeami once talked of art running along parallel lines. Involving other art forms in this process offers a wealth of educational possibilities for the students and for presenting some of the oral histories in alternate ways.

In the Honolulu Theatre for Youth (HTY) project, the students learned basic techniques of two particular types of musical instruments: Japanese taiko drums and the Hawai'ian nose flute. These were chosen initially for their cultural value. As it turned out, these instruments offered a range in volume, texture, mood, and challenges to the students.

Local specialists taught these sessions. Not only did that broaden the theme of *To Feel as Our Ancestors Did*, but students also gained a better understanding of the cultural significance of the music and instruments. We invited dancer/choreographers and musicians into the classrooms for two to four sessions. The guest instructors were given the theme and stories ahead of time so they could tailor their training.

Using music and movement encourages young people to be aware of forms of communication beyond the use of words. Movement encourages them to be precise in their use of gestures and actions and builds a strong sense of ensemble within the students. They learn to depend on each other for coordinated efforts and results.

Building a sequence within a story or scene that combines the use of music and movement is very impressive with young people. Where either the music or movement fails to completely communicate an idea to the audience, a combination often accomplishes the task without having to spell it out. This combination also builds a strong sense of ensemble within the students.

JOURNAL RESPONSE QUESTIONS

A list of potential questions follows. This list was developed over time and with students in Hawai'i. Use as many or as few as apply, and use them as jumping-off points to develop questions more suited to the students involved in the project.

- How did the music/movement classes help you this week?
- What did you do in music/movement class this week that made you proud of yourself?
- When and why did you feel successful with the music/movement?

- When and why did you feel frustrated with the music/movement?
- How did your participation contribute to today's/this week's class(es)? What changes would you like to make for yourself tomorrow/next week?
- In what ways did you actively contribute using the music/movement this week?
- Who in your class made some important contributions using the music/movement this week? What did he do that you felt was important?
- How do you think your class did with the music/movement class this week? What did the class do that was successful? What did the class do that was not so successful? What could your class improve on?

OUTLINE OF THE PROCESS

The music is even more important now because it sets the mood.
—FIFTH GRADER, KANE'OHE

Materials

musical instruments

objects or implements used in the movement sequences

Examples of Instruments

Japanese Taiko Drums

This is a stylistic drumming that incorporates some simple but impressive rituals. Student taiko drums can be easily built from tires, five-gallon paint buckets, clear packing tape, and duct tape (see Appendix Q).

- The power of drums excites students.
- Students easily impress parents with drums.
- The strength of drumming helps clearly define transitions. It can be used for transitions between stories and between classes. Having whole classes exit and enter to drums is an impressive sight.
- High-action scenes such as chases, battles, fires, and other emergencies are well defined by drums and other percussive instruments.

continued

continued from previous page

> *My favorite Taiko drum song goes, bum, bum, bum, bum, tak, tak,*
> *tak, tack. My favorite nose flute tune is [the one] that goes bada, bada*
> *bada, ada, ada, ada, ada, (ata high note,) ada, ada, ada.*
> —FIFTH GRADER, KANEʻOHE

Hawaiʻian Nose Flutes

This kind of flute is similar to a recorder, except it is played with the nose (see Appendix R for examples of making flutes).

- Flutes are great for moods such as sadness, tenseness, calm before the storm, and even agitation.
- When students explore moods through music, they gain more understanding and ownership of a scene.

Found Objects

Found objects give nonmusical students a chance to make music. Objects might include PVC or metal pipe, woodblocks, sticks, garbage can lids, pieces of bamboo, plastic buckets, and wooden dowels. The theatrical model for this is the production of *Stomp!*

- Found objects offer a variety of sound effects.
- A found object ensemble can create moods and underscore action.

Suggested Time Frame

several sessions

What Are You Working Toward?

students experimenting with the range of possibilities offered by the instruments and movement

Music

- Students learn the basic techniques of an instrument or are given found objects and encouraged to experiment with the range of possibilities.
- Individual students are assigned particular parts of scenes or short plays and asked to experiment with sound/music that matches the mood or feeling of the scene/story.
- As the scene is practiced, students apply their experiments.
- The whole group discusses the effectiveness of the music/sound.
- Students redo their music/sound as necessary during further practices.

Movement helps me to understand the story better.
—SIXTH GRADER, KALIHI

Movement

Students learn a vocabulary of gestures and movements and apply them to creating movement sequences for their scenes. Events or environments offer a wide range of possibilities: fires, explosions, airplanes, trains, boats, machines, oceans, rivers, deserts, mountains, forests, rain, blizzards, and floods.

- As a whole group, students learn a wide variety of movements, from walking to running to galloping to twisting to bending to rolling, and so on.
- Groups are assigned parts of scenes or short plays that pose a movement problem.
- Groups brainstorm the use of the movement vocabulary to solve the movement problem.
- The groups develop their movements or sequence of movements.
- Groups share their sequences with the rest of the class.
- The whole group discusses the effectiveness of the movement.
- Groups redo their work as necessary.
- Groups share again and evaluate as desired.

Example

Music and Movement Combination

The oral history informant talked about watching the planes fly overhead, hearing the bombs drop, and seeing people hurt from the explosions during the bombing of Wheeler Air Force base on December 7, 1941.

Students played people walking to church as flute music played. The drums started in softly as the "people" pointed to the sky. The music grew; metal pipes and trash can lids suggested machine guns. The "people" transformed into airplanes. The drumming grew in volume while the "airplanes" transformed into one big airplane. Finally, the drumming came to a clamorous halt as the "airplane" transformed into a bomb. The flutes played softly, suggesting the quiet descent of the "bomb." As the "bomb" hit the ground, the drums played at full force, the bomb "exploding" all over the stage. The instruments and movement stopped. To soft flute music, the students lying about the stage slowly stood, becoming the people who were now hurt and wounded by the explosion.

It was fun for me to be a television. Alex and Kellie are like the television stand. When we do the big fire, we get each other lit by touching knees or legs. We are the fifth group to be lit and do the "shh" sound. I just hope I am not spitting on anyone. So I try to prevent it by swallowing it.

Even though you do the same thing over and over again it is still fun. If you feel tired HTY will surely wake you up because you can use your body parts in all different ways.

—FIFTH GRADER, KANE'OHE

7

Design and Production

I like when we do the transition. I think it is real neat. It's just like magic. The water comes on and it distracts the audience from us and we change the scene into a house and when the last person goes on the water separates. And it is the next scene, just like magic.

—FIFTH GRADER, KANEʻOHE

AT A GLANCE

The drama instructor coordinates the design and building of simple props, costumes, and sets either with other teachers, community/family volunteers, or with the students themselves. The elements are designed to support the imaginative exploration of the process. This keeps the students' and audiences' focus on the scenes, not the "stuff," and keeps control over the size of the performance (and its costs).

GOALS/OBJECTIVES

- to create or find a simple series of set pieces that allow for maximum imaginative and practical use in the production
- to keep the focus of the production on the students and their accomplishments
- to maintain an organizational control of the performance, meaning the many students that must perform a great variety of scenes and get on and off the stage easily and quickly

INSIGHT

This project is about students celebrating their community and exploring their own ability to learn. Overdoing sets, costumes, props, and/or music obscures both the students and oral histories. Parents should leave the performances talking about how much their children achieved, not about the beauty of the background.

In the Honolulu Theatre for Youth (HTY) project, the set included wooden boxes, crates, stepladders, long and wide pieces of lumber, large plastic buckets, five-gallon paint buckets, old tires, and the like. "Rocks" were built from large pieces of styrofoam covered with glue, cheesecloth, and muslin. The objects (or "sittables") were artfully and uniformly painted and arranged in the upstage area for students to sit on while not performing. Students could therefore easily stand and move downstage into the main action of the stories. The various sittables could easily be moved into or out of the action as needed. Realistic props were avoided. Having nearly 150 students performing meant too many small objects that needed to be tracked, watched over, and stored. Instead, simple objects such as poles or pillows were used imaginatively to suggest all implements needed in the scenes.

OUTLINE OF THE PROCESS

Set

The set primarily has three purposes:

- to provide a place on the stage for every student within an individual class to be able to sit throughout their scene or short play
- to have "neutral" objects that could become seats, tables, buses, classrooms, homes, mountains, trees, and so on
- to have a "designed" arrangement of the objects that could become a neutral position so all classes would know exactly where the objects belonged and very little time would be required to reset the stage from one class to the next

I learned performing isn't only if you have the props, I learned it's how you use your imagination!

—SIXTH GRADER, KALIHI

Props

The props should be implements that can be used imaginatively, suggested by the oral histories themselves. For example, if more than one story within an individual class suggests containers or the like, gather a number of buckets for that class and challenge the students to use the buckets as themselves but as other objects as well. Buckets can become steering wheels, chairs, drums, lunch pails, and TVs, among other ideas. If the scenes are about school, use books and rulers. Rulers could be canes, antenna, swords, or even horses. Books might help suggest a fire or be mirrors or shields. Other objects such as umbrellas, brooms, buckets, rope, boxes, wooden picture frames, pillows, and various-sized pieces of cloth can all be put to successful use.

Costuming

If the students simply wear jeans or dark pants, soft shoes, and their school shirt, audiences quickly forget the clothes and focus on the students. The uniformity also gives the production a simple professionalism, as the choice looks deliberate. Using a school T-shirt or uniform helps celebrate the community.

Lighting

Turn the lights on before the show begins and turn them off again when everyone goes home.

Sound

See Chapter 6.

8

Rehearsal Process

*My reaction to today's practice was better than yesterday's practice. I
was thinking ahead this time. When I was performing, it felt like I
was performing in front of a huge audience. In fact, I am going to
perform in front of a live audience. I better get used to it.*
                                        —FIFTH GRADER, KANE'OHE

AT A GLANCE

Individual Rehearsals

Individual classes polish their devised scenes and short plays, adding supporting elements including props, set and costume pieces, music, and/or
other students.

Joint Rehearsals

Individual classes link their scenes and short plays to the other classes that
will be part of the performance and fine-tune basic performance skills. If the
project features a single class or group, then the class focuses on the skills.

GOALS/OBJECTIVES

Individual Rehearsals
- to polish and shape the scenes and short plays in development
- to add musical accompaniment
- to link the small-group presentations through music and narration to
  create a single "unit"
- to begin focusing on performance skills such as projection and enunciation

Joint Rehearsals

- to give classes a chance to see each other's scenes and short plays
- to link separate classes' scenes and short plays into one, seamless performance
- to add musical bridges between separate classes
- to focus firmly on projection and enunciation

INSIGHT

Students need to develop a habit of performing without constant stopping and starting; therefore, a clear deadline should be set to end the devising sequence step and begin rehearsals. Rehearsal sessions should be used to polish the devised scenes and short plays. However, even throughout the rehearsals (and the performances) students should be encouraged to continue exploring and experimenting with new dialogue, getting used to "devising-on-the-spot" without interrupting the flow of performance.

The joint rehearsals bring together the classes that will be performing together (in the HTY project this meant classes within a single grade level). We discovered that the maximum number of classes that should be combined was no more than three in a single performance. Three classes generally meant about forty-five to sixty minutes worth of performance.

The suggested length of the joint rehearsals should include enough time to spend some on practicing basic acting skills (projection and enunciation) and fit in full run-throughs of all the classes. We found, when possible, having individual classes return to their rooms to evaluate their practice and prepare for the next day accomplished a lot more than if all participating classes tried to reflect and evaluate altogether in one room.

If only an individual class has taken on the project, then no joint rehearsals are required. However, the same kind of focus should be placed on this part of the process even if the performance features just a single class. The students' ability to focus on the basic acting skills is greater once they have come to fully understand the oral histories and the structure of their scenes, short plays, and overall performance. The rehearsal period (whether truly bringing classes together or a single class' final rehearsals) is a time for intense, exciting, and joyful practices that lead directly to the excitement of the presentations.

JOURNAL RESPONSE QUESTIONS

A list of potential questions follows. This list was developed over time and with students in Hawai'i. Use as many or as few as apply, and use them as jumping-off points to develop questions more suited to the students involved in the project.

- When I am on stage, I hope that . . .
- How are you feeling about performing? What do you think will happen? How can you best prepare for performing?
- What did you learn in the first part of drama that will help you onstage?
- How did the situation you acted out make you feel and why?
- What part of the scene do you hope to improve on? What are your suggestions?
- How is rehearsing different from drama games and making up the play? Which do you like better and why?
- What do you want the audience to learn from our play? To feel?
- How did the drama classes help you this week?
- What did you do in drama class this week that made you proud of yourself?
- When and why did you feel successful today/this week?
- When and why did you feel frustrated today/this week?
- How did your participation contribute to today's/this week's class(es)? What changes would you like to make for yourself tomorrow/next week?
- In what activities did you participate as a leader this week? What did you do that made you a leader? How did the other students in your group respond to you as a leader?
- Who in your class made some important contributions in class this week? What did she do that you felt was important?
- How well did your group work together this week? What did the group do that you think was good?
- How do you solve problems if your group does not agree? Give an example.
- Did you ever compromise and give up what you wanted to do? How did that turn out?
- How can your group work better as team? What can you do to help the group?
- How do you think your class did in drama class this week? What did the class do that was successful? What did the class do that was not so successful? What could your class improve on?

Individual Rehearsals

> *I found some parts I think we need to work on. Like we need to speak louder and project. I need to work on the flute, that high note I need to play. We could add more stuff to the farm scene so it would not be so boring when we put on a sweater and walk to the farm animals. Because that time no one talks that's why. Also in the hospital scene the need to speak slower and clearer.*
>
> —FIFTH GRADER, KANEʻOHE

Materials

musical instruments, set pieces, props, costume pieces

Suggested Time Frame

The sessions should be flexible in length and duration. Students and groups move at different speeds. Some may need more time to discuss, experiment, reflect, and redo.

What Are You Working Toward?

- students becoming very comfortable with their roles and scenes, aware of what is going on each moment of the play and able to work through mistakes without stopping
- scenes able to run on their own without drama instructor intervention or assistance, ensuring drama instructors will be needed only behind the scenes during the performances
- students consciously improving enunciation and projection

Rehearsal Process

- Have students support each others' scenes by adding musical underscoring or becoming the physical environment (being trees, a forest, the ocean, doorways, other characters in the background of the situation, and so on).
- Put together narrative interludes with the scenes, creating a cohesive whole among the smaller groups within the class and preparing to connect the class with other classes in the grade level or school (as needed).

- Run through the brief plays in their entirety. Groups should be encouraged to improvise their way through mistakes. If students stop every time they make a mistake, they will learn to stop and therefore stop during performance if there is a mistake.
- Run just the tableaux to strengthen them. Tableaux are good anchors for the scenes and short plays. Keeping the tableaux strong and clean gives students control over the beginnings and ends of scenes.
- Begin emphasizing basic performer skills: projection, enunciation, clarity of blocking (when, where, and how actors move on the stage), clarity of music, and choreography.

What the situations of our play made me think about was how tragic the Pearl Harbor bombing was. How it felt when daddies had to leave their families. How it felt when relatives died. It made me feel like I should be thankful for my dad not having to work in the military and that he never has to go to war. Because it made me glad that there isn't a bombing or war right now.

—SIXTH GRADER, KANEʻOHE

Joint Rehearsals

Yesterday we all performed in front of the other fifth graders. We were all mostly nervous to go and perform because it was our first time. Also when we were performing we felt scared because we thought what if the other people don't like it. When I was performing, I felt a little nervous but not too much. I think I did a good job. But I still think I could have done better. Tomorrow I will improve on many different things.

—FIFTH GRADER, KANEʻOHE

Joint Rehearsal Process

- Each day's central goal should be to run through every class' scenes and short plays.
- In the first session, each class shares its presentation with the other classes.
- In the second session, the entrances and exits of each class are staged, adding musical bridges so no break or pause exists as one class exits and the next enters.

- In the third session, a curtain call is staged for the end of the whole presentation. All students within a given grade level are included. The reasons for staging a curtain at the end of the evening rather than after each individual class include:

  It reinforces the unity of the entire project.

  It leaves the audience with a final image of all the participants.

  Parents stay through the program instead of leaving after their child has performed.

- During these rehearsals, place a lot of focus on projection, enunciation, stage presence, and pacing.

- Assign students to sit at the back of the auditorium to monitor other students' volume, enunciation, and positioning (too often facing upstage).

One particular person that I admire in this class is Elizabeth because she is a very soft spoken person. Although when she begins her scene, you see a whole different person who speaks loud, clear, and is very enjoyable to watch.

—SIXTH GRADER, KANEʻOHE

9

Family Night Workshop

Today at HTY [Honolulu Theatre for Youth], we had to show our parents what we were doing. Like tableau and pantomime. Everybody had to go into groups. The people in my group were Lane, Lane's dad, Dane, Alex, Alex's dad, Alex's mom, me and my mom. Each group had to do a little play. Some people had to do plays about family fun and some people had to do plays about chores. We had to do one about family fun.

—Fifth grader, Kane'ohe

At a Glance

Parents, with their children, participate in a hands-on workshop exploring some of the activities the students have been using to devise their scenes and short plays, introducing parents to the process and philosophy of the project.

Goals/Objectives

- to introduce parents to the process of this project
- to introduce parents to a vocabulary of techniques they will see in action in the final performances of the project
- to let students take leadership roles using their newly developed drama skills
- to excite the students and their families about the upcoming performances

INSIGHT

This workshop introduces parents to the process of developing oral history material into a performance, an important step in helping them understand that what they see on performance night isn't just about the final product, but about a way of learning and sharing accomplishments.

The material covered in the family night workshop is material the students have already experienced in class. Therefore, the students take on the role of experts during the workshop. Drama instructors need only introduce each section of the workshop and the students are ready to jump right in, pulling their parents along with them. The parents not only get to see how their sons and daughters are experimenting with and learning valuable skills, but they also get to see their children in action as leaders.

That excitement and the active manner in which the students take the lead impresses parents. The fact that the students interact with their parents in a subject in which they have a greater knowledge and skill excites the students. Overall, it generates an excitement about the upcoming performance and gives students, parents, and teachers a common experience that contributes to a better understanding of the final performances.

Although it can be a little difficult at first getting parents to participate, once the workshop gets under way everyone has a good time. Parents and family members consistently note that participating alongside their children is what makes the workshop so enjoyable. They also note it helps having everyone in the workshop working simultaneously, and alongside other families, and that there is no pressure to perform.

This workshop proved very successful for HTY. One low-income school anticipated that few parents would show up, let alone participate. However, it drew a bigger attendance than any previous parent meeting did. Judging from the laughter and enthusiasm that evening, the interactive nature of the workshop was a key element to the participation.

Some of the principals made the evening a way to reinforce the goals and mission of the school with the parents. They were able to clearly discuss the importance to the school of individual achievement, teamwork, and self-directed learners by drawing references to the activities we did in the workshop. One even had an audiovisual presentation because she did not want to miss the opportunity of educating parents in such an active and entertaining way.

At the end of the workshop parents consistently told us how impressed they were by their own children and how they could already see the effects the project was having on their children's risk-taking, leadership skills, confidence level, and the like. The parents were pleased to have the opportunity to see their children in action, and not just see the resulting grade.

Journal Response Questions

A list of potential questions follows. This list was developed over time and with students in Hawai'i. Use as many or as few as apply, and use them as jumping-off points to develop questions more suited to the students involved in the project.

- How do you think the workshop went? What could improve the workshop?
- How well did your group work together in the workshop? What did the group do that you think was good?
- Which groups worked well together? What did they do that you felt was successful?
- How did the workshop help you?
- Did you participate as a leader? What did you do that made you a leader? How did the others in your group respond to you as a leader?
- What was the most important idea you think your parents or relatives learned in the workshop?
- Having parents/relatives participate in this workshop is important or unimportant because . . .

Outline of the Process

Suggested Time Frame

Sixty minutes

What Are You Working Toward?

- students taking the lead in introducing their family to and guiding them through the drama techniques
- whole families working together
- two or more families working together
- families creating and sharing spontaneously and quickly, having a great time together

Lesson Plan

An outline of the lesson plan is presented here. Complete activity descriptions can be found in Chapter 2.

A. Introduction to the evening

B. Warm-up: body shapes
   1. Individually
   2. As a family

C. Introduce tableau
   1. Autoimages
   2. Spontaneous family group tableaux

D. Family group-created tableaux
   1. Half of the family groups create a tableau titled "Chores"; the other half create a tableau titled "Family Fun."
   2. All family groups practice tableaux once simultaneously.
   3. "Chores" groups share simultaneously, then one group at a time.
   4. "Family Fun" groups share simultaneously, then one group at a time.

E. Introduction of pantomime
   1. Family groups practice on own bringing the tableaux to life through pantomime.
   2. All family groups practice simultaneously once.
      a. Family groups start with their tableau.
      b. On the leader's cue, family groups practice their pantomimed scene.
   3. Individual family groups share one at a time.

F. Introduction of improvisation
   1. Family groups practice their scene again, adding dialogue, sound, and so on.
   2. All family groups practice simultaneously once.
      a. Family groups start with their tableau.
      b. On the leader's cue, family groups practice their improvised scene.
   3. Individual family groups share one at a time.

G. Parting words regarding the classroom and project process and what parents should be looking for when they come to see the final performances

10

Performances

Another thing I noticed was when Danae and the rest of the baseball players was making it up as they go along in the show.
—SIXTH GRADER, KANEʻOHE

AT A GLANCE

Classes perform the short plays and scenes they created for the school and community.

GOALS/OBJECTIVES

- to have the students share their accomplishments with the community and their peers
- to celebrate the community through a unique, community-based event
- to reconnect the students with the oral history informants through the performance

INSIGHT

Once a group of people sits to watch another, a performance happens. How will the audience "see" the performance? In a project such as this one, will they be able to see what the students are achieving or will they see it for what pleases or displeases them? If the audience is not given a context in which to view the performance or are not encouraged to watch for particular actions or achievements, they will experience and respond to the performance in a way they are acquainted with, such as watching TV or seeing a movie. Then

127

they may very possibly walk away saying, "Well, that wasn't very funny," or "They should have painted more realistic settings."

The question then is how can the audiences' eyes be opened to the process the students experience building to and as a part of the performance?

As already noted, the family night workshop is valuable on several levels; parents see their children in action, parents experience their children as confidant leaders as the students easily and willingly jump into the workshop's activities, and all participants develop a beginning understanding of the work, the process, that goes into building toward a performance. When these parents and other relatives attend the performances, they have a more informed eye, seeing within the performance the activities and techniques they explored in the workshop.

Other possible ways to at least introduce the audience to the students' process include showing a "documentary" videotape of the process as a preperformance warm-up for the audience or creating displays of pictures documenting each step in the process.

Each of these choices gives the audience an awareness of the process; however, does it help them see the performance differently? Does the audience know what to look for to see beyond the product to the moment-by-moment accomplishments of the students? Is it possible to create an atmosphere for deeper understanding and appreciation? How can the product be approached as a process of learning for the audience as well?

The answer may lie in questions themselves. As educators we set up certain criteria and questions for students when sharing in-class explorations with each other in order to circumvent and move beyond the simple (and meaningless) "I liked it" or "It wasn't very good" answers. This entire book is dedicated to exploration, reflection, and reexploration, guiding students to take risks and reach inside themselves for deeper understanding and perception. Why not then try the same with the audience?

What types of questions might encourage the audiences to see the processes the students are experiencing within the performance? Here are a select few to stimulate further development:

- What do you see in the action that gives you a sense of the situation, or story?
- When do the students' actions tell the story?
- What emotional quality do the students bring to the situation?
- How committed to the performance are the students?
- How committed to the action does each seem?
- How interested do they seem in the process of performing?

- How strong is their energy?
- Where are the students' focuses?
- How focused are their faces or eyes on each moment or action in the scene?
- How aware do they seem of you, the audience?
- When do they seem to take account of your reactions?
- Where and when can you see the use of techniques?
- Who seems to take the lead in the action or scene?
- How different does your child, student, or brother or sister seem in this performance from what you know of them in daily life?
- What has he seemed to achieve in the performance?

Journal Response Questions

A list of potential questions follows. This list was developed over time and with students in Hawai'i. Use as many or as few as apply, and use them as jumping-off points to develop questions more suited to the students involved in the project.

During the Performances
- How did you feel about performing? How did you prepare for performing?
- What did you learn in the first performances that you used later?
- How did the situation you acted out make you feel and why?
- Which scenes did you improve on?
- How is performing different from rehearsing? Which do you like better and why?
- How did the audience react to your play during the performance? After the performance?

After the Performances
- What did you learn about your community? Your family? Your school?
- When I am old, I really want my grandkids to know about the time when I . . .
- What was the *best* part of the whole drama experience?

  When I am old, I really want my grandchildren to know about the time that I was a bad boy so that they don't get busted from their parents when they are a teenager.

  —Fifth grader, Kalihi

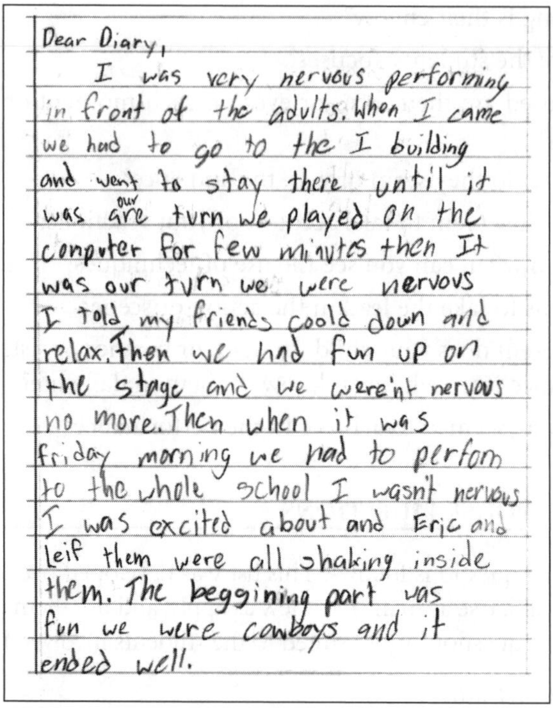

> Dear Diary,
> I was very nervous performing
> in front of the adults. When I came
> we had to go to the I building
> and went to stay there until it
> was our turn we played on the
> computer for few minutes then It
> was our turn we were nervous
> I told my friends coold down and
> relax. Then we had fun up on
> the stage and we were'nt nervous
> no more. Then when it was
> friday morning we had to perform
> to the whole school I wasn't nervous
> I was excited about and Eric and
> leif them were all shaking inside
> them. The beggining part was
> fun we were cowboys and it
> ended well.

Figure 10–1.
Example of student journal entry

OUTLINE OF THE PROCESS

The old people said to me, "Oh, wow, you did a tremendous job. Your great work brought back the old days in me."

—SIXTH GRADER, WAHIAWA

Suggested Time Frame

average of fifteen to twenty minutes per class for an overall running time of about forty-five to seventy-five minutes

What Are You Working Toward?

- bringing together the many contributors to the project: the oral history informants, the music and movement specialists, the school administration, and the parents in celebration of the participating students' accomplishments made through the process

- the sharing of the basic philosophy of the process, guiding the audience to be able to see what kinds of accomplishments the students made

The Performances

The Honolulu Theatre for Youth (HTY) projects always culminated with two performances, one for the school and one for the community. In introducing each performance, the process of the overall project was outlined. For the community performance, we referred to the family night workshop to give families a chance to refresh their understanding of the process as they watched the performances. At the end of the performance, we reminded the audience that the students themselves had imagined and created the presentations they saw, which came as a welcomed surprise to many of the audience members. At one school, the announcement elicited a standing ovation. The performance was appreciated, but the fact the students had created it truly impressed the parents.

We regularly encouraged students to continue improvising, even in the performances. They had tried so many different ways of exploring and presenting the material in their scenes and short plays that we were confident they would not tread into inappropriate or superfluous material. We never had to stop any performance for mistakes, as the students always made their way through any problems. In fact, many students rose to the occasion. Scenes that never seemed to move past a few lines of dialogue became more fully realized in performance, indicating the students were riffing on ideas they had come to fully understand through the process. In one particular case, a scene doubled in length during the performance, without any student missing a beat or getting confused. These discoveries contributed greatly to the students' sense of self and ability.

When first developing the project model, the plan was that classes would perform for each other and a few of the other upper elementary classes. The reasoning was that the content of the performances would make it difficult for lower elementary students. However, after spending such a long time on the project, and particularly because the drumming and nose-fluting had captured the attention of the rest of the school, every class in each school HTY partnered with wanted to see the culminating performance. The younger students responded much in the way the teachers and parents responded; they were intrigued to see their fellow students in a new light.

Students' performing for students is a valuable experience in and of itself. Students watch a performance differently when they are watching their peers. Seeing other students perform can actually inspire young people. This speaks strongly to the students performing for each other even within their own classroom.

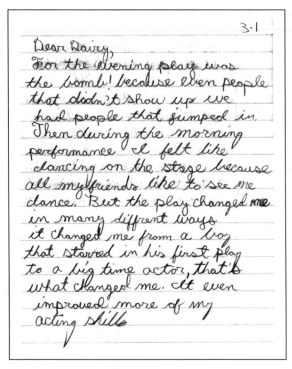

Figure 10–2.
Student journal entry capturing the excitement of the performance

The oral history informants were always invited to the community performance. Without the informants there, the students would have trouble putting the whole process into perspective. Fortunately, the informants' presence also excited the students. The reverse was true as well. The informants got quite a thrill out of the performances. It made their contribution seem more pointed and worthwhile and that they were actively contributing to the education of their communities' youth. One teacher noted that several of the oral history informants still talked about the project and the experience years later. They were touched by the interest shown in their lives and quite pleased how the children put those stories into a performance. In tracking the students' response, many of the young participants began looking at the older people of their community differently. A few even noted they hoped to conduct the same process with their own grandparents, so the stories of old would not be forgotten.

> *I want the audience to feel like they experience WWII again. I want them to feel the fear of it.*
>
> —SIXTH GRADER, WAHIAWA

11

Postproject Reflection and Evaluation

I loved doing this. I learned we can all be loud and get out of our "shells." Drama is good for me because I get out of my shyness, and I also get to work with people. Drama is about changing yourself.
—Sixth grader, Wahiawa

At a Glance

Immediately following and then again several weeks or months after the project is finished, students and teachers assess the project and what they learned about themselves, their peers, drama, community, collaboration, and history through structured activities and questions.

Goals/Objectives

- Students discuss and evaluate the process.
- Students discover what they and their peers best remember from the overall project.
- Students discover what they did that was most effective with audiences.
- Teacher and students explore how drama can be used as a tool for reflection and evaluation.

INSIGHT

Participants of a *To Feel as Our Ancestors Did* project get swept up into the fun and excitement of the performances, making it almost impossible to truly evaluate the overall process immediately following the project. Sharing immediate reactions to the project and then giving everyone time to mull over the experience offers participants a chance to reflect on and evaluate the entire process as fully and objectively as possible. Using the very skills gained earlier in the process, all participants can be involved in an active and engaging evaluation.

OUTLINE OF THE PROCESS

Materials

chart paper, markers

Suggested Time Frame

one or two sessions of forty-five to sixty minutes each

What Are You Working Toward?

- students working together spontaneously to discover which moments in the process, the performances, and the overall project stand out as memorable moments
- students demonstrating a greater understanding of the techniques used during the project
- students working more quickly and with more ease with the techniques
- discovering what most excites and motivates the students in a process such as this

Lesson Plan

An outline of the lesson plans are presented here. Complete activity descriptions can be found in Chapter 2.

Reflection/Evaluation Session for Immediately After the Project

Session

A. Human barometer. (Students agree or disagree with the statements by standing or sitting. Standing indicates an agreement with the statement, sitting indicates a disagreement. If students wish, they may also express subtleties by standing up only partway.)

1. Who felt pleased with their level of participation in . . .
   a. Drama class
   b. Devising
   c. Interviews
   d. Performance
2. Who felt they could have done more in . . .
   a. Drama class
   b. Devising
   c. Interviews
   d. Performance
3. Who would like to do a drama program again?
4. Who learned something valuable?

B. Continuum of achievement. (An imaginary line is drawn from one end of the room to the other. One end of the line means a high degree of participation, the other end, a low degree of participation or none at all. When a statement is read, students place themselves on the line in a place that best reflects their degree of commitment to the stated activity.)

1. When we conducted the interviews, how would you measure your . . . ?
   a. Commitment to asking questions
   b. Using the learning we did in the workshops
   c. Listening
   d. Taking notes
   e. Remembering what the respondents said
2. When we did the drama classes, how would you measure your . . .
   a. Commitment to succeeding
   b. Using the learning
   c. Working with partners (ensemble)
   d. Listening to the leader/each other
   e. Being a leader in the small groups
   f. Risk-taking
   g. Problem-solving
   h. Cooperativeness
3. When we were devising, how would you measure your . . . ?
   a. Commitment to helping create a strong scene

b. Using the learning from drama class

c. Working with partners (ensemble)

d. Listening to the leader/each other

e. Being a leader in the small groups

f. Risk-taking

g. Problem-solving

h. Cooperativeness

4. During the performances, how would you measure your . . . ?

a. Commitment to presenting a strong scene

b. Using the learning from drama and devising classes

c. Working with partners (ensemble)

d. Listening to the leader/each other

e. Being a leader

f. Risk-taking

g. Problem-solving when mistakes came up

h. Cooperativeness

C. Whole-group discussion

1. When you think of this project, what feeling do you get?

2. What special contributions did you make to the project?

3. What do you wish you had done that you did not?

4. What would you do differently if we did the project again starting today?

5. What will you always remember?

6. What surprised you about the stories the respondents told?

7. Which story will you remember most?

8. How are you different from when you started the project?

9. What did you discover about yourself, the school, your community, and/or the world that you never knew before?

10. Who in your class impressed you?

11. Who in your class surprised you?

12. If the principal or superintendent said, "I'm not sure we should ever do drama again. Why should we keep it?" What would you tell her?

13. What could you tell other people about why the project is important to students? To the community? To the people who shared the stories?

14. How does this project help you in other schoolwork? In life?

15. What is happening right now in the world that is like the stories in our play?

D. Small-group brainstorm

    1. Questions to discuss and record

        a. What were your favorite parts of this whole project?

        b. What could this class still do better?

        c. What could be done differently in the future?

        d. What could be added in the future?

        e. What could be taken away in the future?

    2. Groups share and compare answers

Reflection/Evaluation Sessions for Several Weeks After the Project

Session One

A. Warm-up

    A remembered game from the drama classes

B. Discuss

    1. What moments do you remember from the project?

    2. What words or ideas do you remember from the project?

C. Autoimages

    1. Of when you first started this project

    2. Of yourself during the drama classes

    3. Of yourself during the interview process

    4. Of yourself during the process of creating your performance

    5. Of yourself in the performance

    6. After the project was over

D. Small-group tableaux

    1. Re-create your favorite moment in any short play or scene from the project

    2. Share tableaux

E. Reflection on favorite moments

    1. Why do these moments stand out?

    2. What can be deduced from why these moments stand out?

    3. How might the process or performances change based on this new understanding?

Session Two

A. Warm-up

A remembered game from the drama classes

B. Discuss

What makes a good interview?

C. Small-group (five) interview

1. One group member is interviewee, others are interviewers.

2. Interviewers ask questions to find interviewees' most memorable moment from the process of devising and creating the plays.

D. Small-group (five) tableaux

1. The individual interviewees switch to different groups.

2. The groups create a tableau based on the interview (without the interviewee there, so the other students can't rely on them to fill in any undiscovered information from the interview).

3. The groups share tableaux.

E. Reflection on the interviews and personal moments

1. What did you do in today's interview process that used what you learned from before?

2. How did the interviewee feel about the interview? Did the group then capture the moment as you described it?

3. How did the interviewers feel about the interview? How might you change the interview to find out more information?

4. What makes all these moments stand out in our memories?

12

Assessment and Evaluation

What I have to do better for tomorrow is trying to not rush what I am saying. And I want to get more parts. I have only 1 or 2 or 3 parts that I have in my group. And trying to not make it boring because I think most of the students in our class thinks it is boring.
—FOURTH GRADER, KALIHI

AT A GLANCE

Simple surveys, student journals, and teacher observation forms track changes in student behavior, ability, and attitude toward history, elders, drama, and their own sense of self.

GOALS/OBJECTIVES

For Students
- to develop their ability for self-evaluation
- to increase their awareness of what they are learning
- to better understand the choices they and their classmates are making

For Teachers
- to understand how to make the project repeatable
- to help understand the development of each individual child
- to integrate the project with the regular classroom curriculum

INSIGHT

Throughout this book are several excerpts from the student journals kept during the HTY projects. Over the years, we kept evaluating questions and developing new ones, searching for the most concise, thought-provoking questions. These questions reflect those we used most often in the HTY projects. It is by no means complete nor definitive. These give a good indication of the wide range of questions that were developed to track student response on a daily and/or weekly basis throughout the project.

Regularly answered in journals, these questions proved the most insightful way to track the individual students' investment in and reaction to the various stages of the process. For students who did not feel comfortable speaking up in class, it gave them a venue to share their feelings. For the students who liked to speak up in class but often were forced to keep it short due to time limitations, the journals gave them a chance to get it all out.

The downside of these journals is with the students who do not feel as comfortable writing. The journal then becomes an unfortunately frustrating chore that does not truly offer a way to express thoughts about the process. Two possibilities present themselves: one is to design a surveylike journal form that has a select number of questions that will be repeatedly answered throughout the process (giving the students a chance to track their highs and lows, excitements and frustrations, understanding and confusion), the other is to have the students answer the questions into a tape recorder, reading the question first.

Figure 12–1.
Student journal cover

For a view of how student attitudes changed during the process, a pre- and postproject student survey was developed. These surveys, found in Appendix A, tracked attitudes about history, elderly people, and drama.

Listed below is a general outline of the assessment used throughout the Honolulu Theatre for Youth (HTY) projects.

OUTLINE OF THE PROCESS

Forms of Assessment (Copies of the forms can be found in the Appendices)

Pre- and Postsurvey Forms

Before the start of the project and immediately following, students should anonymously fill out the pre- and postsurveys. These surveys track the overall change in student attitude and understanding toward history, elders, drama, and their own sense of self over the course of the entire project.

Teacher/Visiting Artist Observation Forms

The teacher and visiting artists regularly record their observations of individual student and whole-class development.

Journal Entry Forms

The journal entry forms were designed for the students who participated in the annual HTY project to be used in tandem with the journal response questions listed throughout this book. The forms are provided here as a guide for creating journals for (and possibly with) the students. Each step of the process necessitates different ways of evaluating, assessing, and reflecting; therefore, different forms were designed for each specific step. Each of the forms may be used more than once, depending on how often students are encouraged to write in their journals.

- Journal entry (thinking about myself)

  Similar to the survey forms, this one is intended to be filled out both before and after the project.

- Journal entry (question of the day/week)

  This entry form is for use with the journal response questions at each step of the process.

- Journal entry (improving my part) and journal entry (about my group)

  These two entry forms help both individual students and groups regularly reflect on their own work.

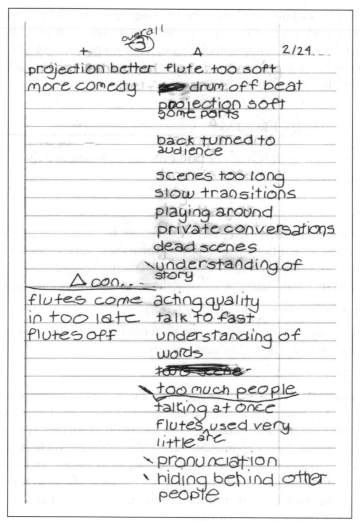

Figure 12–2.
Example of student evaluation of the rehearsals

- Journal entry (improving the scenes)

  When student groups share their developing scenes or short plays for each other, the viewers fill out this form and either read them to or give them to the group that shared.

13

Addressing the Standards

First of all, when we first started our HTY program, I was really shy and only felt like speaking up and expressing myself in front of my friends. I was not used to just letting yourself go and acting things out that you wouldn't normally see people doing. Speaking loudly, expressing myself without thinking, and learning how to do different things, was something I really had to work at. But I now practice these things and have improved a whole lot more than before. I still know that I can work more on just doing it without thinking and expressing myself freely.

—SIXTH GRADER, KANEʻOHE

The Hawaiʻi State Department of Education Social Studies Content Standards state:

> Through enactment of the history, literature, legends, and myths of various cultures, students develop an awareness, appreciation, and understanding of the diverse multicultural society of Hawaiʻi and the world. [Drama] provides a catalyst for the music, dance, story, and visual arts of each culture to come together in a meaningful way.

If every subject area is taught separately, then choices have to be made. Not everything can be done in the short amount of time children spend in the classroom. Therefore, it stands to reason that units of study incorporating more than one subject area or having the potential to interconnect subject areas are preferable. This oral history in performance process offers the potential for connections to many other subjects.

First, this model incorporates the best of both drama and theatre, the process and the product. The many connections that can be made to

143

Drama/Theatre Content Standards are almost too obvious to go into great detail. It is important to note, however, what has been discussed earlier in the introduction: without the time given over to the process of exploring and understanding the techniques used, then the application will be forced and most likely led by the drama instructor, not the students. This is certainly true for any content area. It is why final exams are given at the end of semesters instead of at the beginning. Tests are about applying knowledge. Students need time to be introduced to what it is they are to learn, to learn what they must learn, and to understand what they are learning before they can apply the learning to real situations.

Creating and performing a play is much like the test; it is the structure for the young participants to put their knowledge into action. Therefore ends should not be rushed. It makes no sense to focus on young actors creating perfect tableaux, performing great scenes, or projecting loudly and clearly as they speak on the first (or second or third . . .) day of drama class. They need the time to explore how to perform as much as they need the time to explore the material and shape it into a performance. Choose wisely the content standards being addressed. The journey is more important than the destination.

Drama and theatre, some say, are the synthesis of many arts. Therefore, many other of the Fine Arts Content Standards are addressed here as well, music and dance most directly. They play an important role in finding a well-rounded approach to developing the oral histories into scenes and short plays. How involved those elements become is up to the project leaders, but leaving those elements out both misses an opportunity for enriching the process and the product and addressing those standards actively, with a real purpose that will help the students understand why the standards are important to learn as well as give them the vehicle to apply the learning.

Although not touched on much in this book, visual art can be easily incorporated as well. Everyone is familiar with school performances that involve the young people in the designing and making of set and/or costume pieces.

That, of course, is the key to addressing the content standards. Each aspect of the project needs to be given ample time and focus for the young people to truly gain from this process. Making the young people simply carry out the task of painting does not quite make it. They should be given the time to build ideas based on the oral histories, discuss and develop designs that will serve them both artistically and practically, and discover the optimum ways to carry out their design ideas.

The synthesis does not end there. Drama and theatre, at the very core, are about human behavior and interaction and therefore incorporate many of the basic life skills that parents, teachers, principals, and school systems want their students to master, including oral communication skills, working well with others, risk-taking, reflection and evaluation, and leadership qualities. When the drama process is combined with oral history, learning rises to another level, incorporating a range of curriculum areas, including social studies, language arts, world languages, career and life skills, and even physical education!

Language arts is the most obvious connection. Quoting from the Hawai'i Content Standards, "Language develops from a positive attitude about self as a reader, writer, speaker, and from engagement in meaningful literacy activities. Language enables us to develop social and cultural understanding." In addition, this oral history in performance process and language arts share a similar goal: to develop competent language users who are able to use written and spoken language not only for communication but also for learning and reflection and for social and personal fulfillment and to meet the demands of society and the workplace.

When the students are conducting research to understand the context of the oral histories, they are reading. Developing the scenes and short plays is a long lesson in oral communication and language. Keeping journals is writing.

Social studies are the next obvious connection. Quoting again,

Classroom discussions, collaborative group work, and informal and formal speeches and presentations help students learn to communicate effectively.

The study of culture is more than holidays and food, costumes and crafts. It prepares students to think about culture as a system of beliefs, traditions, etc., and to use that knowledge to celebrate diversity and unity and to develop empathy for people and things different from themselves.

Rather than memorizing names and dates from history texts, students research historical questions, analyze their findings and present them in a form appropriate to class assignments (written, oral, visual, or dramatics). Students conduct oral histories, write firsthand accounts of potentially significant historical events, puzzle over documents and artifacts, research secondary sources, consider the subjective nature of the information they uncover, and interpret information. To construct coherent stories about this collective experience is to create histories.

The connection to content standards goes on, but for now, this short list shows how students can be engaged in learning on many levels through this process. The ideal situation might be to create a wall chart of the content standards. Seeing how the various content standards can be touched on simultaneously could be an exciting learning process in and of itself for students.

Relevant content standards are listed briefly below. These can be consciously incorporated into the process or influence the learning that happens during the project. As each state has its own unique content standards, only a select number of national standards are touched on. As there is much crossover, standards are written out in full only the first time they appear.

National Content and Performance Standards

Drama Skill-Building

Fine Arts—Theatre

- acting by assuming roles and interacting in improvisations
- designing by visualizing and arranging environments for classroom dramatizations
- analyzing and explaining personal preferences and constructing meanings from classroom dramatizations
- understanding context by recognizing the role of theatre, film, television, and electronic media in daily life
  - Students explain how social concepts such as cooperation, communication, collaboration, consensus, self-esteem, risk-taking, sympathy, and empathy apply in theatre and daily life.

Thinking and Reasoning

- applies basic troubleshooting and problem-solving techniques
- applies decision-making techniques

Working with Others

- contributes to the overall effort of a group
- uses conflict-resolution techniques
- displays effective interpersonal communication skills
- demonstrates leadership skills

Interview Skill-Building

Language Arts

- evaluation strategies
- communication skills
- evaluating data
- developing research skills
- participating in society
- applying language skills

Working with Others
- works well with diverse individuals and in diverse situations

Thinking and Reasoning

Collecting Oral Histories

Language Arts

Social Sciences U.S. History Grades 5–12
- era 8: the Great Depression and World War II (1929–1945)
- era 9: postwar United States (1945 to early 1970s)
- era 10: contemporary United States (1968 to the present)

Social Sciences Civics Grades 5–8
- roles of the citizen

Working with Others

Behavioral Studies
- understands that group and cultural influences contribute to human development, identity, and behavior
- understands that interactions among learning, inheritance, and physical development affect human behavior
- understands conflict, cooperation, and interdependence among individuals, groups, and institutions

Thinking and Reasoning
- Effectively uses mental processes based on identifying similarities and differences

Devising Sequence

Thinking and Reasoning

Working with Others

Behavioral Studies

Language Arts
- communication skills
- applying non-English perspectives
- applying language skills

Fine Arts—Theatre

- script writing by planning and recording improvisations based on personal experience and heritage, imagination, literature, and history
- directing by planning classroom dramatizations
- researching by finding information to support classroom dramatizations
- comparing and connecting art forms

Music/Movement

Fine Arts—Dance

- understanding dance as a way to create and communicate meaning
- applying and demonstrating critical and creative thinking skills in dance
- demonstrating and understanding dance in various cultures and historical periods

Fine Arts—Music

- performing on instruments, alone and with others, a varied repertoire of music
- improvising melodies, variations, and accompaniments
- understanding music in relation to history and culture

Rehearsals and Performances

fine arts—theatre

fine arts—dance

fine arts—music

thinking and reasoning

working with others

Family Night

fine arts—theatre

thinking and reasoning

working with others

Appendix A

Student Survey

I work best in a group.
    strongly disagree   disagree   neutral   agree   strongly agree

I cooperate in class.
    strongly disagree   disagree   neutral   agree   strongly agree

I make many contributions to my class.
    strongly disagree   disagree   neutral   agree   strongly agree

I am a leader in my class.
    strongly disagree   disagree   neutral   agree   strongly agree

I like learning about history.
    strongly disagree   disagree   neutral   agree   strongly agree

Learning about history will help me understand life today.
    strongly disagree   disagree   neutral   agree   strongly agree

(City/state) has an important history.
    strongly disagree   disagree   neutral   agree   strongly agree

Elderly people can teach me about life.
    strongly disagree   disagree   neutral   agree   strongly agree

Listening and focusing in class is important.
    strongly disagree   disagree   neutral   agree   strongly agree

I would rather watch than perform.
    strongly disagree   disagree   neutral   agree   strongly agree

I can create characters for a play.

    strongly disagree   disagree   neutral   agree   strongly agree

My class is able to create its own play.

    strongly disagree   disagree   neutral   agree   strongly agree

I believe I can perform on stage in front of an audience.

    strongly disagree   disagree   neutral   agree   strongly agree

Drama teaches me about life and the world.

    strongly disagree   disagree   neutral   agree   strongly agree

Appendix B

Teacher Observation Form

A guide for your personal journal.
Pick one or two areas to address each day.

Date: _____

Observation of students (pick just one or two individuals or make a general note)

Observation of self/interactions

Observation of teaching strategies (successful/not successful) and recommendations

Progress/setbacks/victories

Future sessions: ideas, inspirations, hopes

Appendix C

Visiting Artist Observation Form

A guide for your personal journal.
Pick one or two areas to address each day.

Date: _____

Observation of students (pick just one or two individuals or make a general note)

Observation of self/interactions

Observation of teaching strategies (successful/not successful) and

recommendations

Progress/setbacks/victories

Future sessions: ideas, inspirations, hopes

Appendix D

Postevaluation Guide

Focus of assessment: student achievement, as individuals, as scene/story groups, and as a class

- In what ways did the students take control of . . . ?
  - The overall process
  - The drama techniques and their application
  - The devising process
  - The musical instruments and implementation
  - The performing process
  - The movement ideas and implementation

- To what extent were the students able to . . . ?
  - Carry out the interviews
  - Flesh out the memories into storylines
  - Depend upon themselves for ideas
  - Create scenes from their ideas
  - Invest in the situations they created
  - Overcome mistakes, shyness, internal controversy, and disagreement
  - Listen to each other
  - Work with each other
  - Respond to each other's ideas and contributions
  - Move past the superficial
  - Sustain the commitment to the material, to their ensembles, and to the process
  - Respond to the challenges of performing

Appendix E

Journal Entry

Thinking About Myself

Name: _____ Date: _____

I am best at
(Circle all the phrases that describe you.)

working well with a group   working on my own
listening to others   cooperating in class
making a lot of contributions to my class   being a leader in my class
performing on stage in front of an audience

I am also good at
(Make a list that describes you.)

_____

_____

_____

_____

Drama has taught me
(Make a list that describes what you learned in drama class.)

_____

_____

_____

_____

Appendix F

Journal Entry

Question of the Day/Week

Name: _____ Date: _____

Question of the day/week: _____

_____

My thoughts:

Need more room? Write on the back!
YOU MAY ALSO
Draw a picture of what you learned today on the back.

Appendix G

Journal Entry

Improving My Part

Name: _____ Date: _____

What I did best today or this week was _____

_____

_____

_____

Today I tried to _____

_____

_____

I surprised myself by _____

_____

_____

I think it would be better if I _____

_____

_____

_____

_____

Next time we rehearse I hope to _____

_____

_____

Appendix H

Journal Entry

About My Group

Name: _____ Date: _____

I liked the way _____

_____

_____

_____

_____

I was surprised when _____

_____

_____

I think it would be better if we _____

_____

_____

_____

_____

I think we can make the scene better if we _____

_____

_____

_____

Appendix I

Journal Entry

Improving the Scenes

Name: _____ Date: _____

What was good +	What to work on ▲

Appendix J

Drama Vocabulary

Focus	paying attention to the task at hand
Teamwork/ensemble	working together as a group
Body	a tool of the actor for expression and communication
Voice	a tool of the actor for expression and communication
Imagination	creative center of artists
Tableau	a frozen picture consisting of actors' bodies
Pantomime	the physical expression of an idea; no speaking
Improvisation	creating a scene through dialogue and action without preparation
Character/who	the individuals that inhabit a story
Intention/goal/what	a character's primary want or need
Action	the way a character achieves "want"
Dialogue	the words a character speaks
Conflict	two (or more) characters with opposing wants
Problem/obstacle	what keeps a character from achieving a "want"
Setting/where	where the action of a scene takes place

Appendix K

Drama Vocabulary Posters

These "posters" are used to introduce the drama vocabulary during the drama skills-building workshops. The posters should be hung in the classroom so the students, teachers, and drama instructors can build a shared vocabulary for the devising sequence.

Poster #1

Focus
Teamwork/ensemble

Poster #2

Body/voice
Imagination

Poster #3

Tableau
Pantomime
Improvisation

Poster #4

Character ("who")
    Intention/goal ("what")
    Action and dialogue

Conflict
    Problem/obstacle

Setting ("where")

Appendix L

A Family Story

Who told you the story? _____

Where does the story come from? _____

The title of the story is _____

The main characters of the story are _____

_____

_____

The important events of the story are:

1. _____

2. _____

3. _____

4. _____

5. _____

I think this story is interesting because _____

_____

_____

Appendix M

Making Good Questions

Avoid closed-ended questions.

Did you . . . ?
Do you . . . ?
Can you . . . ?
Have you . . . ?
Are you . . . ?

Use open-ended questions. Start your questions with:

Who . . .
What . . .
Where . . .
When . . .
Why . . .
How . . .

Encourage long *answers.*

Tell me about the . . .
   Best . . .
   Worst . . .
   Most interesting . . .
   Coolest . . .
   Most embarrassing . . .
   Happiest . . .
   Funniest . . .
   Saddest . . .
   Scariest . . .
      experience you had (with your friends, family, in school, etc.)

Use follow-up questions

"What happened before that?"
"What happened next?"
"How were you feeling then?"
"Why did you feel that way?"
"Who else was there?"

Listen, listen, listen to the answers.

If you get a long answer, you scored!

Appendix N

Interview Guide Card

Theme: Topic:

Questions: Follow-up questions:

Golden moments:

Appendix O

Release Form for Interviewee

Name of oral history interviewee: _____

Address: _____

_____

Phone: (   ) _____

Place of interview: _____

Date of interview: _____

I understand that this interview and any photographs, tape recordings, or video recordings are part of a project by students at the school named below. I give permission for the following (check all that apply):

_____ Photos or recordings may be used by _____ school.

_____ Photos or recordings may include my name.

_____ Photos or recordings may be used in a school publication or exhibit related to the project.

_____ Photos or recordings may be used but please do not include my name.

_____ Photos or recordings may be stored for future reading or viewing in the school library.

_____ Photos or recordings may be used, with the following requests or restrictions:

_____   _____

Signature of interviewee   Date

_____   _____

Signature of teacher or principal   Date

Appendix P

Letter to Parents

Date: _____

Dear Parents/Guardians,

Our (grade level or class number) are enjoying a very unique opportunity this school year. We are working on (name of project), a program that offers every student a chance to learn a lot about themselves and (town)'s unique history through a combination of academic subjects, drama, and music.

The project helps our students accomplish many academic goals: practicing writing and reading skills, learning to work together to positive outcomes, to be confident speakers, to ask good questions, to listen well, and to follow directions.

The students have conducted/will conduct interviews with community members. The information the students have collected/will collect in the interviews will be turned into several small shows that include every child in the (grade). These shows will be performed for both our school and for you and your family on (date).

The (school) staff is very excited about this project and hope you will be, too. To make everything work smoothly, we need to get your support and permission to have your child participate in the (month) performances.

Date and Time of Performance

Please contact me with any questions you may have about this project.

Thank you,

_____

Teacher

_____(Student's name) has my permission to participate and perform as a part of the project.

_____   _____

Parent or guardian   Date

Appendix Q

Building a Taiko Drum

You can make a simple taikolike drum with effective sound using an ordinary plastic trash can, a used car tire, or five-gallon paint bucket with 3M packing tape stretched over the open end.

Materials

- the drum

  a plastic trash can, any size (the large thirty-five-gallon size sounds about the same as a medium-size taiko drum), *or*

  a five-gallon plastic paint bucket, *or*

  a used car tire
- clear 2-inch plastic packing tape
- duct tape
- broomstick, or 1-inch round dowel (for the beaters)

Tools

- scissors or X-acto knife
- magic marker
- small saw
- wood rasp or chisel
- sandpaper or a sander

Directions

- **Prepare the bucket/tire**

  Remove labels. Make sure the top edge of the rim is clean and dry. Remove any handles or clips. Make sure the interior is clean, dry, and free of debris.

- **Mark the rim**

  Around the top of the rim, make eight evenly spaced marks. Make the first two on opposite sides, then the next two at 90-degree angles from the first. Finally, make marks halfway between the four previous marks.

- **Make the head: first strip**

  Squeeze the body of the can so the rim is slightly oval. Affix a strip of packing tape across the opening, making sure the mark on the edge is in the middle of the tape's width. Pull it tight, without wrinkles, over to the opposite side. When this first strip of tape is firmly attached and the can released, the rim should look a bit oval shaped.

- **The head: second strip**

  Squeeze the can in the opposite direction so the rim is just slightly oval at right angles to the first direction. This stretches that first strip of tape. Affix a second strip of tape across the opening at right angles to the first strip, using the second pair of marks for alignment. Tack the strips together where they cross. Adjust the stretch so the rim is fairly circular and the tension about equal in all four directions.

- **Test the tautness**

  You should have a cross of clear tape across the top of the can. Lightly tap the center of the cross and listen for the first resonance of the drum's voice.

- **Attach corners**

  Tape strips across the opening from mark to mark until all the marks have a first strip. With each strip, touch down one end, check the alignment, tack down the center, then stretch and tack down firmly, making sure the ends are flat at the rim. You should end up with four strips across the opening. You may want to adjust the tension or tighten the strips at this point. To tighten, detach one end and lift up without detaching the center. Hold the two edges with the thumb and forefinger of each hand, with the rest of the knuckles pressed against the side of the can. Roll both hands back, stretching the tape to the desired tightness. Observe the effect on the other strips; try to equalize the tension.

- **First (radial) layer, first segment**

  Beginning at one of the two original cross-tape strips, attach another strip to the rim on the right side of the first strip, overlapping it at half the width of the tape strip. Pull it across to the opposite side, one-half width to the *left* of the first strip. Stretch it out, tack down the center, and affix the other end at the rim. Repeat with another strip overlapping the last. Continue until you meet the closest initial diagonal strip. You should now have taped in two one-eighth slices of the opening of the can.

- **Radial layer, second segment**

  Rotate the can ninety degrees. Repeat the "attach corners" step for another half quadrant at ninety degrees from the one just completed. The tension on the original four strips will vary and wrinkle slightly, especially if you are making the tape strips nice and tight. This makes a better sound. You will take care of the smoothness of the surface later.

- **Complete the first layer**

  Complete the remaining two half-quadrants. The top is now completely covered.

- **Testing the sound**

  The drum now has a starlike pattern in the center, with a thick center spot. Tap it to sample the sound. However, the edges are thin, with only one thickness at the rim. That is too easy to poke through with a beater.

- **Two parallel layers**

  Starting from the center, stretch parallel, straight, overlapping strips in even rows out to the edge. Make sure they go down flat and avoid trapping air bubbles. Finish the layer by making rows toward the other side. Rotate the drum 90 degrees and repeat the process so you have a double thickness of parallel strips at right angles to each other. The additional layers add strength to the head. If applied carefully these layers flatten the surface of the head and cover wrinkles that may have developed due to the changing tensions in applying the first layer. Because the tape sticks to the layers below, they will vibrate as a single head.

- **Reinforce the edge**

  Trim overexcess tape from the sides of the can. About two to four inches down the side is plenty. Seal down the tape ends along the rim with one or two wraps of duct tape around the side of the drum.

- **Bashi (beaters)**

  Cut the broomstick or dowel into lengths 12 to 18 inches long. Round off the ends and sand smooth; make sure there are no splinters. Make them good and smooth.

- **Try it out**

Appendix R

Building a PVC Flute

Materials

- One- to three-foot PVC quarter-inch pipe
- PVC corner piece
- pencil
- drill with one-eighth bit *or* hammer and nail

Directions

- Attach the corner piece to the straight pipe.
- Hold pipe in your hands.
- Have a friend mark off where your fingers are.
- With the drill or hammer and nail, make holes at the marks.
- Only make holes on one side.

Play

- Blow into the corner piece. Take fingers off the holes and you get different notes.
- Find the highest note you can make. Find the lowest note you can make.
- Experiment. Try making a different flute with shorter or longer piping.

Appendix S

Building A Bamboo 'Ohe-hano

The Hawai'ian Nose Flute

The 'ohe is made from bamboo cut ten to twenty-one inches in length. A natural node, or closing, is left at one end with the other end left open. The diameter is generally from one to one and a half inches.

Materials

- bamboo, preferably the green variety as opposed to the yellow
    one to one and a half inches in diameter
    a single section of bamboo about ten to twenty inches from node to node
- hacksaw
- hand drill with quarter- or half-inch bit
- small round file
- sandpaper

Directions

- Cut the bamboo. Be careful not to crack it as that destroys the tone.
- Drill the nose hole to fit. Have the player place the closed end under the nose and twirl the bamboo to find a comfortable position. Mark where the nose is. Drill as close as possible to the inner side of the closed end.
- Drill the finger holes according to comfort.
    The space between the nose hole and the first finger hole is usually about five inches.
    The finger holes are generally an inch apart, although they should be spaced to fit a comfortable spread of fingers for the player. Some make flutes with as many as five holes, although three offers a good range and ease of play.
    The holes are about a third of an inch in diameter.
    The shorter the flute and the closer the holes, generally the easier it is to play.
- Sand or file the holes and the area around the holes to create a smooth surface and ensure comfortable fingering.

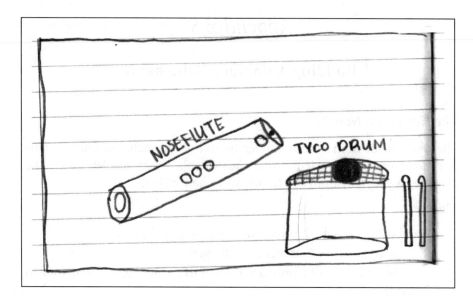

Play

There are many ways to hold an 'ohe while playing. Generally, whatever is most comfortable is the correct position. It may be held in the left hand, the left thumb pressing the left nostril closed with the right hand free to finger the holes. Left-handed players may wish to reverse this procedure.

Honolulu Theatre for Youth (HTY) Participant Reflection

Excerpts from Student Journals

I prefer HTY more than recess.

—*FIFTH GRADER, KANEʻOHE*

Self-Awareness

HTY has made me speak louder and it helps when I have to do my book report, so that I can get a good grade. So far, ever since the play I have gotten A's on all my book reports since then. Speaking louder will also help me in the future so that I can good grades, get into a good college, get a great job and last but not least, be the best that I can be.

—*SIXTH GRADER, KALIHI*

I believe that HTY has made me become more of a free and happy person because of Miss Tracy. She does not only tell us what to do, but she explains it well and also acts it out to give us ideas on how to do it or what we can do.

—*SIXTH GRADER, KANEʻOHE*

I think my imagination has gotten better because instead of having scripts to memorize we think of things off the top of our heads.

—*SIXTH GRADER, KANEʻOHE*

I want to continue the play with all my heart. You don't know how sad I'm gonna feel when the play is not going to happened. Every day after drama class, I always think what I'm gonna do about drama, not anything else. And if this play won't work, what about those hard work I put just to keep this play going. Am I just going to throw all that away?

—*SIXTH GRADER, KALIHI*

Sometimes when we get a group and we had our idea, I feel nervous and stupid. But if you just stand there doing nothing, they'll laugh anyway. It's better to laugh with them and do it, or they'll laugh at you when you don't.

—*SIXTH GRADER, KANEʻOHE*

Engagement in Learning

I want this to continue. This makes me feel like I can do anything.

—*Sixth grader, Kaneʻohe*

Today at HTY we ran through the whole play. It was kinda cool. I added in a new line.

—*Fifth grader, Kaneʻohe*

Sept. Entry —And I really hate drama it really stinks.

Dec. Entry —The first time we had Drama we use to hate it but now we love doing it.

March Entry —I would love to put on another play. Because it's fun and funny. We should probably put on a play of Peter Pan. Maybe the end of the school year?

—*Sixth grader, Kalihi*

Practice at recess, practice over the weekend, practice on my own, and committed!

—*Fifth grader, Kaneʻohe*

I think we should do this in 7th grade because we still can learn more about Wahiawa.

—*Sixth grader, Wahiawa*

Group Awareness

I think Chris is a good role model for the class because he cooperates with anybody and no matter what happens he does great. The reason why he does great is because he just throws himself into the play and, if he makes a mistake he just keeps going.

—*Fifth grader, Kaneʻohe*

From Miss Kuraoka's class I admire Dana. She acted like a real naughty kid but in real life she doesn't really act like that. She acts so naughty I couldn't believe it.

—*Fifth grader, Kaneʻohe*

One thing that I learned was that it's mainly about cooperation. Without each other's support we would all be still planning. The other thing that I learned was that putting a play together is very fun! I thought it was one of the most funnest things I ever did.

—*Sixth grader, Wahiawa*

Self-Assesment

The hardest part of our play is when Mr. Lopez becomes an angel because it doesn't really look like an angel. Also my voice doesn't sound like an angel. Ms. Tracy can you give me some advice on making myself an angel. How can I make my voice?

—*Sixth grader, Kaneʻohe*

I need to work on talking instead of being a scarecrow that has no mouth. If I try better our scene will be much better than it is now.

—*Sixth grader, Kaneʻohe*

Today for HTY I think we didn't do too well practicing. Today I felt like we failed to practice. We took too long to get set up. Dan had to tell us what to do. I felt that we could have done better. But other than that we did pretty good. Next time we practice, I think we can do a whole lot better.

Today for HTY we did a lot better than yesterday. Dan even said so. I think we will be ready to perform in front of the school. We did better than some of the fifth grade classes. The only thing that we need to improve on is talking loud.

—*Fifth grader, Kaneʻohe*

I want to change my shyness, talkingness and just work on talking less and be more open on shyness. Also leaning against something and include some boys in our group. And don't hog all the ideas because no one will want me in their group.

—*Sixth grader, Kaneʻohe*

The thing about being a log is that you need to hold on to the cloth good because if we don't then it won't look like a log and it will look like a weird thing falling down on the ground and everyone will be wondering what is the cloth fall down for and then they won't like the log people.

—*Fifth grader, Kaneʻohe*

Application of Skills and Knowledge

But when I saw the news yesterday they said that Iraq was bombed. I wonder why do they fight. I wish they would just stop fighting and be friends like in Hawaiʻi.

—*Sixth grader, Kaneʻohe*

I think that HTY helped me a lot to speak loud and clear. Especially when we give our book reports, they require a visual report a written report and an oral. When we give our oral reports, we have to compete with the lawn mowers outside. Because of HTY, when I speak people in the back of the room don't have to strain their ears just to hear me.

—SIXTH GRADER, KANE'OHE

Teamwork was also one of the things we have been working on. This was a very simple thing for me because I sit on a table with all boys and sometimes you just have to learn that sometimes your best decision is to just go along with their suggestions, even though you don't agree with them.

—SIXTH GRADER, KANE'OHE

Empathy

I also really like it because it really reminded me of how they lived when they were young. The way they used light is they had to use a lantern. They had to do lots of chores and they always did their homework at night.

—SIXTH GRADER, KANE'OHE

Letters of Support from Teachers and Principals

Wahiawa (1997–1998)

When we first began discussing this project with Dan Kelin from HTY, our plan was to include the students in grades four, five, and six. We really had no idea what we were getting into. However, as the project developed, we included a member of the Wahiawa Centennial Celebration Committee, became more focused, and worked toward a performance deadline. When the monies became available, we decided to work with only the fifth- and sixth-grade students.

Before beginning the first phase of the project, which was collecting oral histories, the teachers needed to be in-serviced by Warren Nishimoto from the University of Hawai'i's Oral History Department. As teachers, we were overwhelmed with the actual processes involved and needed to streamline the steps for our students. The students practiced interviewing each other, taking notes, and writing short biographies of each other. They learned to write interview questions and to talk story. They had to learn how to operate the tape recorders and transcribe the interviews. When they were ready, they were grouped by threes and fours. Two days were set aside for the interviews.

We took some of them to the Wahiawa Museum—The Land of a Million Pines to gain background information about Wahiawa. We researched Wahiawa's history with several books, photos, and old calendars.

The children asked grandparents, neighbors, family members, and community senior citizen groups to assist with the oral history interviews. Many of our old-timers were too humble, too shy, or unable to communicate with our students. When we finally had enough interviewees, we were ready to begin.

We collected/borrowed tape recorders from the entire school and a few students brought some from home. We then had to find places to interview all of these people. Every available space was utilized. The teachers provided refreshments and the school donated pencils, school pins, portfolios, and lunches for the interviewees.

The interviews were tape-recorded, but the students also took notes. They then had to meet in their groups to transcribe their interviews and word process all of their oral histories. When the rough drafts were completed, they were turned over to Dan and Tracy from HTY. They scanned the material for possible dramatization ideas.

For two weeks in December, the children were taught various theatre vocabulary and techniques. This background-building proved to be invaluable. The students thoroughly enjoyed this phase.

Beginning in January, we began on the actual stories shared in the oral histories. When more information was needed, our interviewees met with the students again, or answered the questions on the telephone. Many different scenes were acted out by the students and dialogue added.

Resources such as movement, taiko, and nose flute were brought in to enhance the performances. The playing of Hawai'ian instruments added another dimension.

Without the leadership and guidance of the two resources from HTY, Dan and Tracy, this project would not have attained its highly polished performance.

As teachers, we learned to step back and listen and learn along with our students. It was very difficult for us to just assist when needed. Many times we found ourselves ready to discipline or begin giving students dialogue or movements to do. It was a very humbling experience for us. We learned to put our complete trust in Dan and Tracy. After all, they had done this kind of project before and we were the novices.

The students learned so many things, especially the importance of working together, making sure that whatever needed to be done got done. They proved to themselves that they were capable of speaking loudly, acting out parts, stepping in when someone was absent, knowing where to be when offstage so that they would be in the right place for the next scene, and so on.

As the date of the performance got closer, many of the students wanted to know if their interviewees would be in attendance. They wanted them to see their stories dramatized because they were proud of what they were doing. They had somehow bonded with their interviewees. The students gained an appreciation of their elders and what they had experienced.

The interviewees who were present at the evening performance were so moved by the students' reenactment of their lives. Many stopped to congratulate us, as they were leaving, saying that the plays had brought back so many memories for them.

The students were so proud of themselves following the two performances. It's something they will remember for the rest of their lives. There was a lot of family bonding and pride evidenced by the large turnout of family members.

History is now something they can relate to. Collecting oral histories has made them more aware of how their parents and grandparents have lived.

Thank you for allowing us the privilege of working with you on this marvelous, worthwhile project.

—*GRADE 5 CHAIRPERSON*

Kaneʻohe (1998–1999)

To the Samuel N. and Mary Castle Foundation

Our school just completed one semester with the Honolulu Theatre for Youth residency entitled Oral History/Living History Program. We were absolutely thrilled with the results of this residency as it provided opportunities for our students to apply skills learned and achieve our learner outcomes. It also created opportunities for students who wouldn't ordinarily excel in our academic curriculum a chance to be showcased. It was especially satisfying to see students who were the quiet, shy types blossom and assert themselves on stage. This very fact has caused two grade levels to rethink their gifted and talented performance arts program to include all students in the finale instead of only a select few.

The students who participated in this program slowly evolved into confident oral communicators after the artists' gained their trust and shared their passion for improvisation. They were challenged to become self-directed learners, complex thinkers, and collaborative workers when presented with scenarios that required them to stop, think, and react. They were forced to be creative as quality producers and effective communicators because the artist kept asking for "what other way or how else could you show. . . ." Ordinary objects such as rope, buckets, brooms, and pillows became articles of clothing, transportation vehicles, or furniture. Students learned how to read each other, develop a sense of timing, and "feed" each other lines. They learned how to be respectful, resourceful, and responsible as a member of a scene. The relationships that were developed will last them their lifetimes. Without any hesitation, I would welcome any opportunity to collaborate with HTY in the future. This approach accommodates the learning styles of our kinesthetic learners while making learning fun for all.

Thank you for this opportunity to partner with the Honolulu Theatre for Youth. The Samuel N. and Mary Castle Foundation has definitely changed our thinking about the importance of using the arts to enhance literacy.

SINCERELY,

PRINCIPAL, KANE'OHE

Kalihi (1999–2000)

Aloha,

I am a sixth-grade classroom teacher in Kalihi. Through our school's data gathering from student and parent questionnaires, student interest inventories, and observations of students by our staff, we determined that the majority of our school population learns best through hands-on, interactive activities. For that reason, we have tapped the talents of our multitalented students, seeing them excel in the areas of art expression (drawing, painting, music, and drama). My experiences with another theatre company and with that of HTY has led me to believe that unless you have qualified instructors having the background in stage and/or theatre performance (such as those hired by HTY) as well as the ability to maintain classroom control of students, student outcomes will not be as rich as it could be.

I have been very satisfied with the services rendered to my students each year that I have contracted services from the Honolulu Theatre for Youth. They are able to provide me with a preplanning conference, where we address my needs as well as those of my students, review my thematic curriculum plans, remain flexible throughout their servicing of my class to adjust their instruction to match the needs of my students, and ask that I complete a daily critique of their work session with my students.

This year was no different. My students and I were fortunate enough to be offered an opportunity to work in-depth with HTY covering a progressive five months, which included planning, learning/revisiting drama skills, learning how to perform oral history interviews, doing the actual interviews on selected members in our community, suggesting and creating scenes using tableaux and improvisations, then putting together the actual stage performances. From the very beginning, I asked that my students maintain a diary to reflect on their thoughts and feelings throughout this exciting journey. I utilized this journal as one of the means for assessing the program.

I am able to see positive gains in academic areas such as in reading, writing, oral communication, their ability to work cohesively on group projects, and in their social interactions with their peers and adults when I compare their performances at the beginning of the school year with that of present. More of my students have become risk-takers and have been readily volunteering within the class and school as participants for activities.

HTY has been an integral part of our community, providing quality stage productions for thousands of public school students at affordable prices. Their reputation is unquestionable and so too their school residencies, which is in addition to their stage productions. Our partnership with HTY has assisted us in meeting the performance standards and expectations of our students.

I truly support the Honolulu Theatre for Youth in its quest to reach out to students and our communities but they depend heavily on donors to make it all materialize. Many of us wish we could take our students to see Broadway plays or be swept off our feet with the musical numbers many of our mainland counterparts have available to them. The Honolulu Theatre for Youth attempts to expose us to the classics, the analogies of life, oral histories of diverse cultures, and provides opportunities for us to use our imaginations where we can pretend to be specific characters in different time periods or to be something we are not.

Seeing things from different perspectives or points of view has taught students to review all facts before making judgments against others. It has always been a good reminder for myself, too. This has helped avoid heated arguments between my students when they utilize strategies in conflict resolution, make wiser choices, and discuss alternatives and possible solutions to their problems. These are strategies taught and reinforced by the Honolulu Theatre for Youth. Yes, there are very few programs out there to help support our school standards and curriculum in the way they do. I do a lot of curriculum integration and the Honolulu Theatre for Youth's approach is exemplary with an excellent working relationship with the schools and the communities. I strongly support their presence in the schools and in communities.

SINCERELY,

SIXTH-GRADE TEACHER

To whom it may concern,

I am a fourth grade teacher. The population of students here are "at-risk" children. Thirty-two of my students participated in the HTY oral history project this year. I strongly feel that this project was an educational and a personal growth experience for my students and that drama is an excellent way to bring learning alive. I have used several techniques/skills that HTY developed with my students; they were able to perform the drama task as they learned other content areas. It helped them to visualize what they were learning.

At first, my students needed to feel more comfortable in taking the risk in performing in front of their peers. It was stressful in the beginning but at the end of the project, students were very confident and felt sad that it was coming to an end. They learned a lot and worked very hard. They now try to use their questioning skills on me when they want to stall for time or to get me to tell them more about myself. Overall, I have seen positive changes in my students; they seem more confident and have grown closer as a group. The play forced them to develop skills for the real world. They needed to take on challenges such as asking good questions to get a story, speaking in front of a large audience, projecting their voices, working together, taking risks, being focused, and enjoying the experience.

The project has also enhanced my curriculum; I've tried to use more drama skills in helping the students to visualize what they are reading and feeling. In writing, a journal was kept to document their thoughts and ideas as they went through the whole process. Both group and individual oral reports are done with confidence.

The time and preparation spent on this project were well spent. The interviewee for our play was our librarian. She was very touched and it brought back fond memories of her childhood. For any student to develop social, communication, and emotional skills through this oral history project is priceless. I really believe that when they look back on their experience in elementary, this oral history project will be one that they will remember. We were fortunate that we were able to participate in this project and look forward to working with HTY again in future projects.

SINCERELY,

FOURTH-GRADE TEACHER

Dear Dan,

I am writing to thank you for the work that you did in my fourth-grade class and for my school with the oral history drama project.

Whenever I have had drama in my classroom in previous years, I had always thought that the time, usually one-week residencies, was too short to make a tangible impact. In this oral history project, there was enough time for the students to have an experience that they will remember for the rest of their lives. The experience of hard work and teamwork resulting in a visible, tangible, exciting product—the play on stage for an audience— is an invaluable lesson for them.

The students loved drama. For some, especially those who are not academically brilliant, this was a chance to show a different kind of brilliance. They were given a chance to shine.

I have many examples of shining moments, from the girl who became more in control of her emotions to be one of the storytellers, to the one who struggles in reading and math but proved to be gifted and talented in creative movement, to the boy who became connected and confident enough to be chosen as the grade-level announcer. I could go on and on. I do believe that the greatest impact on this class this year was that they all grew in self-confidence. They almost all stated that they learned to speak louder and that they had less fear on stage.

Besides reaching all the drama standards, the project was most relevant to language arts curriculum, particularly speaking, listening, and writing. The interview process was an integral part of the project and helped the students to develop speaking and listening skills. Writing in their journals was a natural extension to the activities and most students found this enjoyable. After the interviews, we wrote thank-you notes to our informants. From these letters, I was able to assess how much they learned from the informants and how well they were listening. Some of the students had the opportunity to develop musical skills and talents, with the drums and nose flutes. We also learned about life in different places and different eras, and we compared and contrasted some relevant aspects of the oral histories. We also submitted short paragraphs to the parent bulletin in October, based on the stories they had collected from their families.

I read somewhere that more than anything, to be prepared for the future, students of today need to learn how to collaborate with others. The fact that ensemble building and teamwork was difficult in my class underscores how important it was that we did it. We did the hard work, the laying down of a foundation, for a process that hopefully will be built upon in the years to come.

For me, as an individual, I have long been interested in learning more about using drama in the classroom, mainly for the experience of artistic collaboration that I am familiar with as a playwright. I admit to lacking the skills and confidence required to undertake a project of this scope by myself. I have learned a lot from you this year, and I hope we can continue to work together in the future.

—Fourth-Grade Teacher

Bibliography

Drama

Boal, A., and A. Jackson, trans. 1992. *Games for Actors and Non-Actors.* New York: Routledge.

Johnstone, K. 1999. *Impro for Storytellers.* New York: Routledge.

Kohl, H. 1988. *Making Theater: Developing Plays with Young People.* New York: Teachers & Writers Collaborative.

McCaslin, N. 1990. *Creative Drama in the Classroom.* New York: Longman.

————. 2000. *Creative Drama in the Classroom and Beyond.* New York: Longman.

Neelands, J. 1990. *Structuring Drama Work: A Handbook of Available Forms in Theatre & Drama.* Cambridge: Cambridge University Press.

O'Neill, C., and L. Johnson. 1984. *Dorothy Heathcote: Collected Writings on Education and Drama.* Cheltenham, UK: Stanley Thornes Ltd.

O'Neill, C. 1995. *Drama Worlds: A Framework for Process Drama.* Portsmouth, NH: Heinemann.

Rohd, M. 1998. *Theatre for Community Conflict and Dialogue: The Hope Is Vital Training Manual.* Portsmouth, NH: Heinemann.

Saldana, J. 1995. *Drama of Color.* Portsmouth, NH: Heinemann.

Spolin, V. 1986. *Theater Games for the Classroom: A Teacher's Handbook.* Evanston, IL: Northwestern University Press.

Tarlington, C. 1995. *Building Plays: Simple Playbuilding Techniques at Work.* Portsmouth, NH: Heinemann.

Tarlington, C., and P. Verriour. 1991. *Role Drama: A Teacher's Handbook.* Portsmouth, NH: Heinemann.

Walker, P. 1993. *Bring in the Arts: Lessons in Dramatics, Art, and Story Writing for Elementary and Middle School Classrooms.* Portsmouth, NH: Heinemann.

Weigler, W. 2001. *Strategies for Playbuilding.* Portsmouth, NH: Heinemann.

Stories

Barton, B. 1990. *Stories in the Classroom: Storytelling, Reading Aloud, and Role Playing with Children.* Portsmouth, NH: Heineman.

Cooper, P. 1993. *When Stories Come to School.* New York: Teachers & Writers Collaborative.

Dyson, A. H., and C. Genishi, eds. 1994. *The Need for Story: Cultural Diversity in Classroom and Community.* Urbana, IL: National Council of Teachers of English.

Zipes, J. D. 1995. *Creative Storytelling: Building Community Changing Lives.* New York: Routledge.

Oral History

Akeret, R. U., with D. Klein. 1991. *Family Tales, Family Wisdom: How to Gather the Stories of a Lifetime and Share Them with Your Family.* New York: Morrow.

Brown, C. S., 1998. *Like It Was: A Complete Guide to Writing Oral History.* New York: Teachers & Writers Collaborative.

Center for Oral History. 1985. *How to Do Oral History.* University of Hawai'i. (You can obtain a copy by calling 808-956-6259.)

Davis, D. 1993. *Telling Your Own Stories: For Family and Classroom Storytelling, Public Speaking, and Personal Journaling.* Little Rock, AR: August House.

Davis, O. L. Jr., T. Sitton, and G. L. Mehaffy. 1983. *Oral History: A Guide for Teachers.* Austin: University of Texas Press.

Davis, S. and B. Ferdman. 1993. *Nourishing the Heart: A Guide to Intergenerational Arts Projects in the Schools.* New York: City Lore, Inc.

Greene, B., and D. G. Fulford. 1993. *To Our Children's Children: Preserving Family Histories for Generations to Come.* New York: Doubleday, 1993.

Hickey, M. G. 1999. *Bringing History Home: Local and Family History Projects for Grades K–6.* Boston: Allyn and Bacon.

National Endowment for the Humanities. 1999. *My History Is America's History,* Guidebook. (You can obtain a copy by calling 1-877-NEH-HIS-TORY or at www.myhistory.org.)

Perl, L. 1989. *The Great Ancestor Hunt: The Fun of Finding Out Who You Are.* New York: Houghton Mifflin.

Perlstein, S., and J. Bliss. 1994. *Generating Community: Intergenerational Partnerships Through the Expressive Arts.* New York: Elders Share the Arts.

Rogovin, P. 1998. *Classroom Interviews: A World of Learning.* Portsmouth, NH: Heinemann.

Winston, L. 1997. *Keepsakes: Using Family Stories in Elementary Classrooms.* Portsmouth, NH: Heinemann.

Zemelman, S., P. Bearden, Y. Simmons, and P. Leki. 1991. *History Comes Home: Family Stories across the Curriculum.* York, ME: Stenhouse.

History/Social Studies

Jorgensen, K. 1993. *History Workshop: Reconstructing the Past with Elementary Students.* Portsmouth, NH: Heinemann.

Schmidt, P. R., and A. W. Pailliotet. 2001. *Exploring Values Through Literature, Multimedia, and Literacy Events: Making Connections.* Newark, DE: International Reading Association.

Steffey, S., and W. Hood, eds. 1994. *If This Is Social Studies, Why Isn't It Boring?* York, ME: Stenhouse.

Oral History Collections

See, L. 1996. *On Gold Mountain: The One-Hundred Year Odyssey of My Chinese American Family.* Vintage Books.

Terkel, S. 1986. *Hard Times: An Oral History of the Great Depression.* New York: Pantheon Books.

———. 1997. *The Good War: An Oral History of World War Two.* New York: New Press.

Websites

Australian Oral History website: www.museum.vic.gov.au/hidden_histories/classroom_materials/oral.htm

CARTS, Cultural Arts Resources for Teachers and Students: www.carts.org

Louisiana Voices, an educator's guide to exploring our communities and our traditions: www.louisianavoices.org

National Content and Performance Standards: www.mcrel.org/standards-benchmarks

National Endowment for the Humanities: www.myhistory.org

Smithsonian Center for Folklife and Cultural Heritage: web2.folklife.si.edu